A JOURNEY INTO
CHINA'S ANTIQUITY

A JOURNEY INTO CHINA'S ANTIQUITY

National Museum of Chinese History

Volume Two

Warring States Period

Qin Dynasty

The Western and Eastern Han Dynasties

Three Kingdoms through Western
and Eastern Jin to Northern and
Southern Dynasties

MORNING GLORY PUBLISHERS

Editor-in-Chief: **Yu Weichao**

Managing Editor: **Xiao Shiling**

Conceived by: **Yan Zhongyi**

Editor: **Zheng Wenlei**

Chinese text by: **Wang Guanying, Wang Zhiben, Chen Chengjun,**

Wang Yonghong, Lai Guolong, Shao Wenliang, Shao Xiaomeng

Translators: **Gong Lizeng, Yang Aiwen, Wang Xingzheng**

Photographers: **Yan Zhongyi, Sun Kerang**

Assistant Photographers: **Shao Yulan, Liu Li, Dong Qing**

Maps by: **Huang Yucheng, Zhang Guanying, Zhang Jie,**

Duan Yong, Zhu Yongchang

Designer: **Zheng Hong**

A JOURNEY INTO CHINA'S ANTIQUITY

Volume Two

Compiled by:

NATIONAL MUSEUM OF CHINESE HISTORY

Published by:

MORNING GLORY PUBLISHERS

35 Chegongzhuang Xilu Beijing 100044 China

Distributed by:

ART MEDIA RESOURCES, LTD.

1507 South Michigan Avenue Chicago IL 60605 USA

Tel: 312-663-5351 Fax: 312-663-5177

First Edition First Printing 1997

ISBN 7-5054-0483-0/J·0200

37400

Printed in the People's Republic of China

Contents

Warring States Period

(475-221 BC)

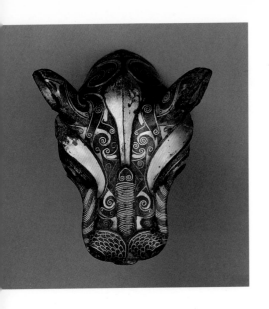

Two events marked the beginning of the period in Chinese history known as the Warring States: usurpation of government power in the state of Qi by the Tian family and division of Jin into the three states of Han, Zhao and Wei. It was a period of incessant wars, but also one of rapid growth on the economic and cultural fronts. The feudal system was in a dominant position by this time, and the new mode of production it established was in an ascendant stage. The rulers of the feudal states, to maintain themselves and contend with each other in wars of annexation, had to develop production on a large scale and strengthen their economic position.

The new social system and the expanding economy broadened humanity's vision and in a large measure emancipated the mind. A profusion of new ideas and new schools of learning emerged to meet the needs and challenges of the new era. Exploring anew the mysteries of the universe and the philosophy of life quickly became the vogue, and the different schools vied with each other in proclaiming new philosophical and political theories so that in the ideological realm a lively situation described as "a hundred schools of thought contending" prevailed.

In the realm of art there was also unprecedented vitality and enthusiasm with music, dancing and the plastic arts all advancing in giant strides. Medicine and the natural sciences also made new progress with discoveries and inventions far ahead of achievements in other parts of the world. The strengthening of economic and cultural intercourse between different regions and the consequent integration of different nationalities laid the foundation for the eventual establishment of a unified country.

Coexistence of Seven Powers

The seven largest states of the Warring States Period were the Qi, Chu, Yan, Han, Zhao, Wei and Qin. These seven states waged fierce wars with each other, grabbing land and cities in order to extend their domains. They had to strengthen themselves economically and militarily, and to do this needed to institute various legal and social reforms. Qin, in the west, became more and more powerful and in the course of time was able to annex the six states in the east.

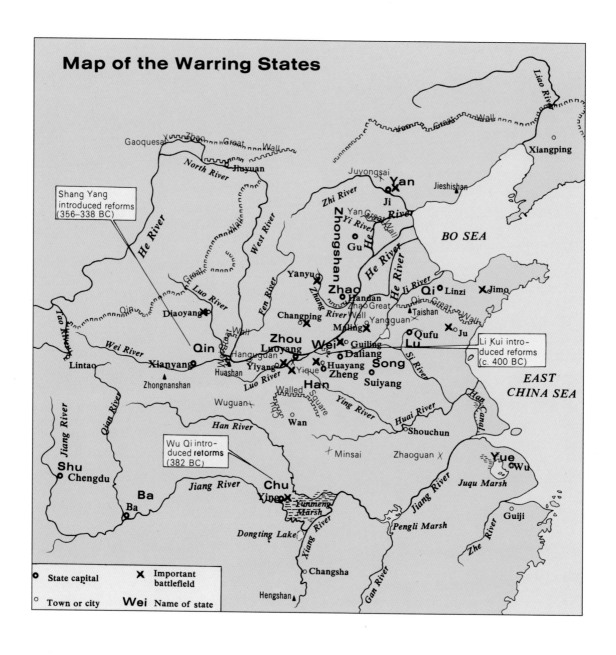

Map of the Warring States

Shang Yang introduced reforms (356–338 BC)

Li Kui introduced reforms (c. 400 BC)

Wu Qi introduced reforms (382 BC)

● State capital   ✕ Important battlefield

○ Town or city   **Wei** Name of state

l. Bronze horsehead with gold and silver inlay   Ornament on shaft of carriage, relic of Wei, Warring States Period; unearthed at Guwei Village, Hui County, Henan Province, in 1951. It is 8.8 cm high, 13.7 cm long, and has a neck diameter of 4.8 cm. The head and neck are inlaid with gold patterns shaped like fins and curled hair. Exquisitely wrought, it is a typical example of bronze objects inlaid with precious metals of the Warring States Period. Wei was a large aristocratic family of the state of Jin during the preceding Spring and Autumn Period. Gradually it became a powerful political force. In 471 BC, the Wei and two other powerful families, the Han and Zhao, after eliminating all other contending forces, divided the state of Jin between themselves (historians call this episode "Three Families Divide Up the Jin"). In 403 BC, King Weilie of Zhou made a vassal state of Wei which thereafter became a powerful feudal state of the Central Plains. Its territory covered the southwestern part of present-day Shanxi Province and the northern part of Henan Province. In the beginning its capital was at Anyi (now Xia County, Shanxi). Later it moved its seat to Daliang (now Kaifeng, Henan). In the early years of the Warring States Period, Marquis Wen of Wei appointed capable ministers like Li Li, Wu Qi and Ximen Bao, who enacted economic, political and military reforms that speeded up the feudalization of Wei, turning it into a powerful and prestigious state. The tomb at Guwei Village, Hui County, is a large-sized structure (with two tomb paths) shaped like the Chinese character for middle (中). It is surrounded by a cemetery of the scale of a feudal lord's mausoleum, which apparently is why the shaft ornament recovered from it is of such elaborate workmanship.

1

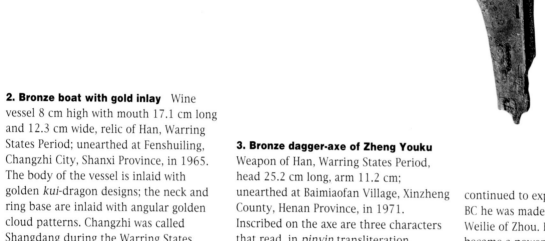

3

2. Bronze boat with gold inlay   Wine vessel 8 cm high with mouth 17.1 cm long and 12.3 cm wide, relic of Han, Warring States Period; unearthed at Fenshuiling, Changzhi City, Shanxi Province, in 1965. The body of the vessel is inlaid with golden *kui*-dragon designs; the neck and ring base are inlaid with angular golden cloud patterns. Changzhi was called Shangdang during the Warring States Period. It was located near the juncture of the three states of Han, Zhao and Wei. Because of its importance politically and militarily, the Han regime made it an auxiliary capital. Fenshuiling Cemetery is on the northern outskirts of Changzhi. It is a spacious piece of land that must have been the burial ground of important rulers of Han, for many exquisite objects have been unearthed there.

3. Bronze dagger-axe of Zheng Youku Weapon of Han, Warring States Period, head 25.2 cm long, arm 11.2 cm; unearthed at Baimiaofan Village, Xinzheng County, Henan Province, in 1971. Inscribed on the axe are three characters that read, in *pinyin* transliteration, "Zheng Youku." Zheng, or Xinzheng, was the capital of Han. It is now part of Xinzheng County, Henan Province. Youku (literally "Right Storehouse") was a Han department where weapons were made and stored. Han was originally the name of a senior official of Jin during the Spring and Autumn Period. He became a powerful political figure who eventually took part in carving up Jin and then continued to expand his territory. In 403 BC he was made a feudal lord by King Weilie of Zhou. His fiefdom, called Han, became a powerful state of the Central Plains during the Warring States Period. Its territory covered the southeastern part of what is now Shanxi Province and the central part of Henan Province. Its capital was originally at Pingyang (now Lingfen, Shanxi). Later it was moved to Yiyang (now Yiyang County, Henan) and then to Yangzhai (now Yu County, Henan). Finally, after Han conquered the state of Zheng, it made Xinzheng its capital.

4. Bronze vessel cast by the son of the Squire of Linghu   Wine container of Han, Warring States Period, height 46.5 cm, mouth diameter 14.8 cm; said to have been unearthed in Jin Village, Luoyang, Henan Province, in 1927. The cap is ornamented with six flaps resembling lotus petals. The body is circumscribed with five rows of coiled-dragon patterns, separated from each other by narrow grooves. On the neck is an inscription of 50 characters in 23 lines, an eulogy by the son of the Squire of Linghu to mark the casting of the vessel. Linghu is located to the southwest of Yishi County, Shanxi Province. In the early Warring States Period, the ruler of Jin granted one of his senior officials a fief, and gave him the title of Squire of Linghu.

5. Clay vessel with animal-shaped ears painted in red Wine container of Yan, Warring States Period, 70.2 cm tall; unearthed in Songyuan Village, Changping County, Beijing Municipality, in 1964. It is made of gray pottery with mud content and had a roughcast of dark gray and a flat top. The neck of the vessel is square and the shoulder and belly are round. On two opposite sides of the neck are symmetrical animal-shaped ears; on the other two sides are rings dangling from the mouths of animal masks. The shoulder and belly of the vessel are divided into four parts by wide ridges and decorated with cloud and variant coiled-dragon designs painted red. Attractively shaped, this vessel is a rare object among ceramics of the Warring States Period. Quite a few painted clay vessels that are imitative of bronze have been discovered in and around Shangdu (southwest of Beijing) and Xiadu (now Yi County, Hebei) of the ancient state of Yan. Evidently, burying such objects with the dead was a Yan funeral custom.

5-1

◁ 5-2

6. Zihezi's bronze *fu* (caldron)   Measuring device of Qi, Warring States Period, 38.5 cm high, mouth diameter 22.3 cm, capacity 20,460 ml; said to have been unearthed at Lingshanwei, Jiao County, Shandong Province, in 1857. On the body of the measuring device is an inscription of 9 lines, recording Zihezi's promulgation of standards of volume. The gist of the inscription is: "Zihezi has ordered that Chen De be informed to the following effect: The granary *fu* shall be the standard unit for all *fu* measures, and the granary half-*sheng* [*sheng*, a traditional unit of measurement] the standard for all *zhi* measures. If any official attempts to cheat, he must be stopped. If he does not stop, he shall be punished according to the seriousness of the offense." Zihezi was the official title of Tian He when he was a senior official of Qi during the early Warring States Period. Later this same Tian He usurped power and became the ruler of Qi. He was made a vassal lord by King An of Zhou in 386 BC. As this *fu* was cast before that occurred, it must have been cast sometime between 404 and 385 BC. It is a typical measuring device of the Warring States Period, and shows that the state of Qi had a strict system of measures at the time.

6

7. Bronze lamp with human figure Relic of Qi, Warring States Period, height 21.3 cm, diameter of each plate 11.5 cm; unearthed at Gebukou Village, Zhucheng County, Shandong Province, in 1957. The lamp consists of a human figure holding in each hand a branch with a plate on top. The figure stands on a coiled dragon. The plates are attached to the branches by tenon and mortise and can be freely removed. The lamp was unearthed together with a bronze spoon for adding oil. In the early years of the Western Zhou, Qi was a large state ruled by a family with the surname Jiang. In 481 BC, Tian Heng (or Tian Chengzi), a high official, staged a coup. He made Duke Ping the nominal ruler but held all power himself. Then, in 386 BC, his great-grandson Tian He deposed Duke Kang and made himself ruler of Qi in both name and deed. Thereafter Qi was ruled by the Tian family. Qi was a large state whose territory covered most of present-day Shandong Province, plus southeastern Hebei Province. Bordering on the sea in the southeast, it had access to ample resources of salt and fish and was the richest of the seven Warring States. Its capital was Linzi (to the west of what is now Zibo Town, Shandong).

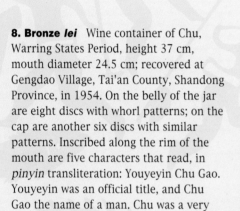

8. Bronze *lei* Wine container of Chu, Warring States Period, height 37 cm, mouth diameter 24.5 cm; recovered at Gengdao Village, Tai'an County, Shandong Province, in 1954. On the belly of the jar are eight discs with whorl patterns; on the cap are another six discs with similar patterns. Inscribed along the rim of the mouth are five characters that read, in *pinyin* transliteration: Youyeyin Chu Gao. Youyeyin was an official title, and Chu Gao the name of a man. Chu was a very large state. Its territory extended from the eastern border of what is now Sichuan Province and covered the whole of Hubei Province, northeastern Hunan Province, northern Jiangxi Province, northern Anhui Province, southern Henan Province, the middle part of the area north of the Huai River in Jiangsu Province, and the southeastern corner of Shaanxi Province. Its capital was originally at Ying (now Jinan Town, Jingsha City, Hubei). Later, menaced by Qin, it moved its capital to Chen (now Huaiyang, Henan) and then to Shouchun (now Shou County, Anhui), its power and influence gradually diminishing in the process.

9. Bronze dagger-axe with brocade design Weapon of Chu, Warring States Period, 24 cm long; said to have been unearthed at Changsha, Hunan Province. There are four holes on it. Both sides of the head and arm are decorated with diamond-shaped brocade patterns, exquisitely carved. Studies show that brocade patterns of such high quality were executed by a special method that used copper sulphide. Weapons treated in this way were not only attractive in appearance but also rust-proof. They reflect the high level of China's smelting and founding techniques in those faraway times. Of the seven Warring States, Chu was militarily the strongest rival to Qin's efforts to unify the country. Having occupied the states of Wu and Yue of the Spring and Autumn Period, it acquired many famous swords and had a highly developed weapons industry. This exquisitely wrought dagger-axe was not used by soldiers or junior officers; it must have been the weapon of a high ranking officer. Actually two such dagger-axes were unearthed at the same time; presumably they were a pair.

10

10. Bronze tiger tally Transportation certificate of Chu, Warring States Period, 12.4 cm long, 7 cm high, 0.5 cm thick; said to have been unearthed in Shou County, Anhui Province. Tallies were needed to transport or move troops, to enter or leave passes and courier stations, and to collect taxes. When used, a tally was split into two halves, the two parties concerned each holding one half. A tally would not be considered valid unless the two halves matched. The one shown here is shaped like a tiger. On the obverse side is an inscription that reads in translation: "King's Order: Lend." It meant that the king ordered all courier stations to provide horse, chariot, food and drink to the bearer of the tally when he passed. As Shou County was at one time the capital of Chu, it is not strange that a tally issued by a king of Chu should be unearthed there.

11. Bronze crouching ox with silver inlay Object for weighing down a mat, 10 cm long, 5 cm high, Chu relic, Warring States Period; unearthed in Shou County, Anhui Province, in 1956. On the body of the ox are cloud patterns inlaid with silver. Under the belly is an inscription that reads in translation, "Article of the Dafu." The Dafu was a department somewhat like a treasury in the king's palace. Apparently this bronze ox was an article kept in the Dafu for the use of the royal family, which is why it was so beautifully wrought.

11

12-1

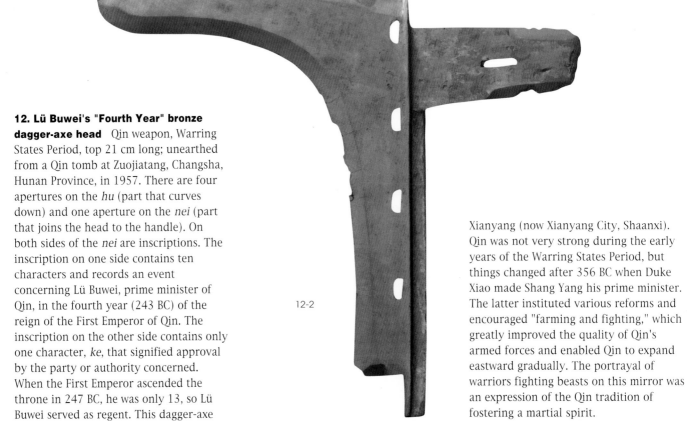

12. Lü Buwei's "Fourth Year" bronze dagger-axe head Qin weapon, Warring States Period, top 21 cm long; unearthed from a Qin tomb at Zuojiatang, Changsha, Hunan Province, in 1957. There are four apertures on the *hu* (part that curves down) and one aperture on the *nei* (part that joins the head to the handle). On both sides of the *nei* are inscriptions. The inscription on one side contains ten characters and records an event concerning Lü Buwei, prime minister of Qin, in the fourth year (243 BC) of the reign of the First Emperor of Qin. The inscription on the other side contains only one character, *ke*, that signified approval by the party or authority concerned. When the First Emperor ascended the throne in 247 BC, he was only 13, so Lü Buwei served as regent. This dagger-axe was cast during his regency.

13. Bronze mirror with figures of warriors fighting beasts Qin relic, Warring States Period, 10.4 cm in diameter; unearthed from a Qin tomb at Shuihudi, Yunmeng County, Hubei Province, in 1975. The mirror has a two-layer square knob. On the reverse side is a pattern of fine lines serving as the background. Carved upon this background are two warriors each with a shield in the left hand and a sword in the right, fighting two fierce leopards. Realistically and meticulously portrayed, they reflect

12-2

the militant spirit of the Qin people. During the Warring States Period, Qin was a large state on the western border of the country. Its territory extended from the southeastern part of what is now Gansu Province, along the Wei River, to the heartland of present-day Shaanxi Province. Its capital was originally at Yong (now Fengxiang County, Shaanxi). Later it moved its seat to Jingyang (north of present-day Jingyang County, Shaanxi), then to Liyang (north of present-day Fuping County, Shaanxi), and finally to

Xianyang (now Xianyang City, Shaanxi). Qin was not very strong during the early years of the Warring States Period, but things changed after 356 BC when Duke Xiao made Shang Yang his prime minister. The latter instituted various reforms and encouraged "farming and fighting," which greatly improved the quality of Qin's armed forces and enabled Qin to expand eastward gradually. The portrayal of warriors fighting beasts on this mirror was an expression of the Qin tradition of fostering a martial spirit.

13-1

13-2

Economy of the Warring States Period

The establishment of the feudal system and the reforms undertaken by the various states led to rapid development on the economic front. Agricultural production increased and brought unprecedented prosperity to merchants and artisans. With the development of trade, cities that were once political and military citadels now became industrial and commercial metropolises, the economic centers of different parts of the country.

Extensive Use of Iron Tools

Improved iron-smelting techniques and the extensive use of iron tools were important to the country's rapid economic development during the Warring States Period. Great progress was made in the techniques for casting pig iron and smelting iron ingots mixed with carbon to make steel. Pig iron products treated for malleability possessed the properties of both hardness and softness, the two complementing each other. Sharp, tough and tensile iron tools helped improve agricultural techniques and were used to carry out intensive cultivation, dig ditches, build dams, undertake large water conservancy projects, and raise the output of handicrafts, during and after the mid-Warring States Period.

Sites Where Ironware of the Warring States Period Was Unearthed

14. Map of sites where ironware of the Warring States Period was unearthed
Important handicraft centers for iron smelting were set up all over the country during the Warring States Period. Iron implements and weapons dating from this period have been unearthed in the former territories of all seven of the most powerful states. They have also been found in places once inhabited by the Huhe people in the north and the Hundred Yues in the south. Altogether nearly a thousand pieces of ironware have been recovered to date, including farm tools, handicraft tools, miscellaneous objects and weapons, the most numerous being farm and handicraft tools. Among the most significant discoveries were 87 iron molds, comprising 51 sets, unearthed at the site of a Yan foundry in Xinglong County, Hebei Province; 80-odd iron implements recovered from Yan ruins at Lianhuabao, Fushun, Liaoning Province; and 58 farm tools found buried around five Wei tombs in Hui County, Henan Province.

15. Map of water conservancy projects of the Warring States Period Such projects included building dams, digging canals, and other engineering works for the utilization of water resources. Large-scale dam building took place mostly in the three states of Qi, Zhao and Wei, which were located on the middle and lower reaches of the Yellow River; the purpose was to prevent the river from flooding. Digging canals had begun during the last years of the Spring and Autumn Period. In 486 BC the state of Wu built a city at Han (northwest of present-day Yangzhou City, Jiangsu) and dug a canal, also called Han, to link the Huai and Yangtze Rivers. Later, it built a canal from the Huai River to the states of Qi and Lu, joining the Huai with the Ji and Si rivers. During the Warring States Period, Ximen Bao, magistrate of Ye County (southeast of present-day Ci County, Hebei) of Wei, to improve the irrigation of farmland, ordered the construction of a project to "divert water from the Zhuang River to irrigate Ye." Later, during the reign of King Hui of Wei, a canal was built that brought water from the Putian River (west of present-day Zhongmou County, Henan) to the northern walls of Daliang (now Kaifeng, Henan). Subsequently this canal was extended from Daliang to Xing (north of Xingyang County, Henan), a project that not only diverted water from the Yellow River to the Ying River but made possible through water transportation between the Yellow River and the Huai. The whole length of the waterway was called Honggou, or the Hong Canal. During the reign of King Zhao of Qin, Li Bin, prefect of Shu (now Chengdu, Sichuan), built a dam across the Min River to the west of Guan County— "a dam in midstream" for the purpose of diverting water. Floodgates were installed to control the flow, which not only prevented flooding but benefited both irrigation and navigation. During the last years of the Warring States Period, Qin built the Zhengguo Canal, which brought the waters of the Jing River from Zhongshan (northwest of present-day Jingyang County, Shaanxi) westward to the Luo River, a distance of 150 kilometers, to provide much needed irrigation for the dry plains of Guanzhong.

16. Mold for casting two sickles simultaneously Yan tool, Warring States Period, 32 cm long, 11.3 cm wide; unearthed at Gudonggou, Xinglong County, Hebei Province, in 1953. This mold with a bow-shaped handle on the back can cast two sickles at the same time. Near the handles of the sickles are two characters that read in *pinyin* transliteration, "You Lin," which was the title of the official in charge of casting. Iron tools were widely used during the Warring States Period, and the principal tools were for farming. This led to the rapid development of both agriculture and the handicrafts, which in turn expedited the development of the feudal economy.

16

Map Showing Water Conservancy Projects of the Warring States Period

Legend:

○ **Han** Feudal state and its capital
○ Community center
Marsh
Major irrigation area
Major water conservancy project

15

Bronze Casting

Bronzes of the Warring States Period included fewer ritual vessels but a larger number of articles for daily use, whose designs tended to be more and more realistic. By this time it was already possible to make use of a variety of techniques such as split-mold casting, welding and die casting. Crafts requiring fine workmanship such as engraving, inscribing, mounting, inlaying and gilding also reached new heights.

17. Table showing the compositions of six kinds of bronze objects   The ancient writing *Kao Gong Ji* (A Study of Handicrafts) contained a summary of bronze making in China during the pre-Qin period. It listed the proportions of different metals in six kinds of bronze objects. Bells and tripods contained six parts of copper to one part of tin, which works out at 85.71% copper and 14.29% tin. Axe heads contained five parts of copper to one part of tin, or 83.33% copper and 16.67% tin. The heads of dagger-axes and halberds contained four parts of copper to one part of tin, or 80% copper and 20% tin. Blades of knives, swords, etc. contained three parts of copper to one part of tin, or 75% copper and 25% tin. Arrowheads contained five parts of copper to two parts of tin, or 71.43% copper and 28.57% tin. Mirrors and flints contained equal parts of copper and tin.

Bells, Tripods	Axe Heads	Dagger-axes	Blades	Arrowheads	Mirrors
Cu 85.71%	Cu 83.33%	Cu 80%	Cu 75%	Cu 71.43%	Cu 50%
Sn 14.29%	Sn 16.67%	Sn 20%	Sn 25%	Sn 28.57%	Sn 50%

18

18. Bronze mirror with coiled-dragon openwork   Chu relic, Warring States Period, 20.5 cm in diameter; unearthed from a Warring States tomb at Zhangjiashan, Jiangling County, Hubei Province, in 1976. This mirror consists of a surface of silver white mounted on a piece of openwork. At the center of the openwork is a small round knob with a hole through which a ribbon could be passed. Around the knob is a pattern of coiled dragons, and along the rim is a circle of diamond-shaped openwork. Bronze metallurgy was well developed in the state of Chu. Many bronze mirrors have been unearthed from what used to be Chu territory. They were varied in style, exquisitely wrought, and beautifully designed. In shape, they were of two main categories, round and square, round mirrors being more common. The knob on the back was rather small and it usually had a three-string pattern on it.

19. Bronze mirror with six-hill pattern

Relic of the Warring States Period, 23.2 cm in diameter, 0.6 cm thick along the rim. It has a knob in the center, around which are six figures, evenly distributed, resembling the Chinese character for hill. Between the "hills" are dense patterns of clouds and leaves serving as the background. Mirrors with "hills" were popular during the Warring States Period, from Yan in the far north to Chu in the south. They were most numerous in the state of Chu where three-hill, four-hill, five-hill and six-hill varieties were cast. Most of the mirrors that have been unearthed had three-hill or four-hill patterns. Six-hill mirrors are rare, and the one shown here is the most beautiful of all.

19-1

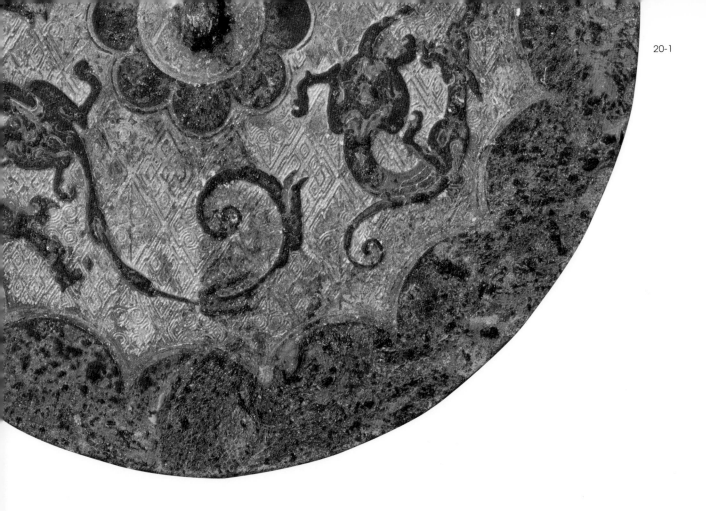

20. Bronze mirror with 16 arcs and 3 animal images Relic of the Warring States Period, 14 cm in diameter, 0.2 cm thick along the rim. There is a round knob at the center, surrounded by a pattern of petals. Along the inside of the rim is a circle formed by 16 arcs of equal length joined to each other and curving inward. Within this circle of arcs are the images of three heavenly beasts with coiled bodies and long tails, vivid lifelike creatures that seem to be flying. Casting bronze mirrors has had a long history in China. They have been discovered among the ruins of the Qijia culture in Gansu Province. However, bronze mirrors dating from the Shang-Zhou dynasties are few and are usually small in size. They began to appear in larger numbers during and after the Warring States Period, and were of very high quality in terms of workmanship and decoration.

20-2

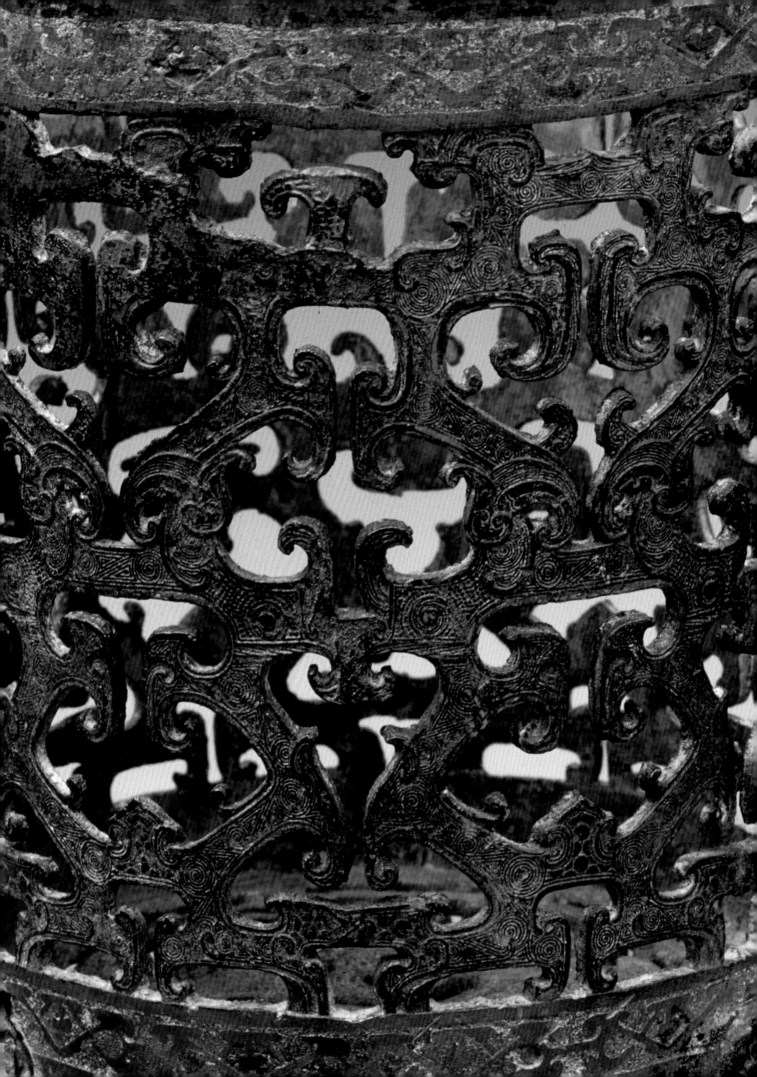

21. Bronze *lian*, openwork with animal design Chu relic, Warring States Period, 14 cm high; unearthed at Xiaoliu Village, north of Changtai Pass, Xinyang, Henan Province, in 1957. The vessel is shaped like a brush holder with three legs and a slightly enlarged mouth, and is decorated with an openwork of deformed animal images and inlaid with turquoise, A *lian* was for holding a lady's toilet articles in ancient times. This one, however, with a

21-2

large mouth and small bottom and decorated with openwork, was probably made for a different purpose. Making openwork objects of bronze was a traditional craft of Chu. Objects of this kind that have been discovered in China include mirrors, caskets, cups, and even some large-sized implements, all of exquisite workmanship.

◁ 21-1

22. Bronze jar Zeng wine container, Warring States Period, height 124.5 cm, mouth diameter 48.4 cm; unearthed from Tomb 1 at Leigudun, Sui County, Hubei Province, in 1977. The cap, on which there are four rings, is connected to the jar by a chain attached to an arched dragon-shaped knob on the shoulder. There are four more rings on the body, which presumably were for tying ropes to move the jar. On the neck and lower part of the body are patterns shaped like plantain leaves, composed of figures resembling coiled serpents. Encircling the middle part of the body are three rows of patterns also with figures resembling coiled serpents. On the neck is an inscription of seven characters that says the jar was a large wine container in the house of Marquis Yi of Zeng. It is the largest bronze jar yet discovered in China and the largest bronze object of the Warring States Period.

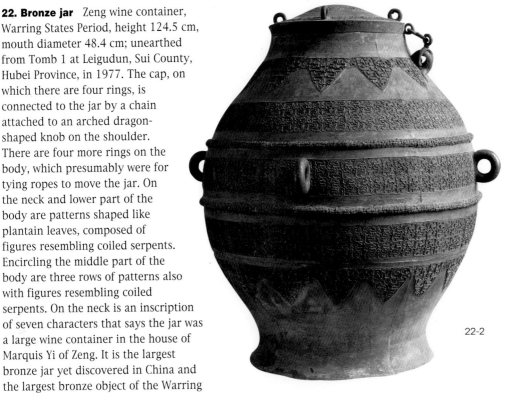

22-2

23. Bronze halberd with three hooks Zeng weapon, Warring States Period, 3.43 meters long (including shaft); unearthed from Tomb 1 at Leigudun, Sui County, Hubei Province, in 1978. The shaft is made of wood wrapped in slips of bamboo tied securely with silk threads and coated with lacquer. It is straight and strong, smooth and resilient. Below the bronze spike are three hooks, the first two 4.7 cm apart, the second and third 5 cm apart. The first hook is provided with a *nei* (a short end that protrudes beyond the opposite side of the shaft). A long weapon with a spike and three hooks like this one was evidently made for chariot fighting. It was the first time that such a weapon had been discovered in China. Tomb 1 at Leigudun was the tomb of Marquis Yi, ruler of Zeng, a state of the early Warring States Period. Many exquisite relics have been recovered from his tomb.

◁ 22-1

23

24

24. Bronze *jian* (ice box) Vessel to ice wine, 76 cm long on each side and 63.2 cm high, Zeng relic, Warring States Period; unearthed from Tomb 1 at Leigudun, Sui County, Hubei Province, in 1978. It is a square box with a square *hu* (flask) inside. It has a cover of openwork, at the center of which is a square hole that fits exactly around the square mouth of the *hu*. The *hu* has a cap, sloping shoulders, and a body whose lower part curves inward. Its base is pierced with holes. The bottom of the *jian* is fitted with hooks at places corresponding to the holes in the *hu*, and they are inserted into the holes to keep the *hu* steady. One of these hooks is provided with an inverted hook; when the hook is inserted in the hole, the inverted hook drops automatically like a tightening device to hold the *hu* securely in place. On the body and four corners of the *jian* are eight ears shaped like dragons. Above the head of each dragon is a bronze piece resembling roof eaves. The four legs of the *jian* are shaped like animals. The four sides are decorated with openwork and cloud-and-coiled dragon designs in relief. People in those days drank rice wine, which would overferment and turn sour if kept too long. This *jian* was made to keep the wine in the *hu* cool with ice cubes so that it would last longer without losing its taste. A spoon with a long handle, obviously for stirring the wine, was unearthed together with the *jian*.

25-1

25. Bronze tripod of Xiong Han, King of Chu

Chu ritual vessel, Warring States Period, 55.6 cm high; said to have been unearthed at Lisan Gudui, Zhujiaji Village, Shou County, Anhui Province, in 1933. Inscriptions on the cover and body say that the vessel was cast by Xiong Han, King You of Chu (reigned 237—228 BC), from metal obtained after destroying and melting weapons captured in war. Shou County was the capital of the state of Cai in the early years of the Warring States Period and was called Xiacai at the time. After Cai was conquered by Chu, the name of the county was changed to Shouchun. In 241 BC, King Kaolie of Chu (called Xiong Wan), threatened with invasion by Qin, moved his capital to Shouchun and renamed it Ying. Xiong Han was Xiong Wan's son. He was buried at Shouchun and this tripod was discovered at the site of his grave.

26. Ejun Qi's gold-inlaid bronze tallies

Permits for land and water transportation in Chu, Warring States Period; unearthed from Qiujia Garden, east of Shou County, Anhui Province, in 1957. Tallies were of two kinds, for vessels and vehicles respectively. To be used, a tally had to be divided into two halves, the two parties concerned each holding one half. A tally would not be considered authentic unless the two halves fitted exactly. The tally for vessels (right) is 30.9 cm long, 7.1 cm wide and 0.6 cm thick. It bears an inscription of 165 characters in 9 lines inlaid with gold. The one for vehicles (left) is 29.6 cm long, 7.3 cm wide and 0.7 cm thick and has a gold-inlaid inscription of 150 characters. The inscriptions tell us that King Huai of Chu gave the tallies to a man called Ejun Qi in 323 BC and they mention in detail the routes he was to take, the kinds and quantities of goods he was to carry, and the tariffs to be paid. They provide valuable data for the study of the geography of Chu and its transportation and tariff systems.

25-2

26

Lacquerwork

Lacquer wares of the Warring States Period included wood carvings with lacquer painting and objects surfaced with lacquer on a base of bamboo, wood, skin or ramie. They were usually brightly colored and vividly decorated. Lacquer vessels with an inlaid metal hoop around the mouth appeared during the late Warring States Period. This technique not only produced more durable articles but enhanced the decorative effects.

27. Lacquered cup with ears Zeng wine cup, Warring States Period, 4.2 cm high, mouth 14.6 cm long and 11 cm wide; unearthed from Tomb 1 at Leigudun, Sui County, Hubei Province, in 1978. This is a wooden cup coated with black lacquer on the outside and red lacquer inside. The rim and ears are decorated with black cloud designs. Many lacquer vessels were unearthed from the tomb, all of exquisite workmanship, since they were the funerary objects of a feudal lord.

28. Small black lacquer table with vermilion designs   Furniture of the Warring States Period, 40.5 cm high, 57 cm long, 10 cm wide. It is a small, attractive wooden table used as a support and is coated with black lacquer on which are painted vermilion designs. Making lacquerware is a Chinese craft with remote traditions. It appeared as early as the Neolithic Age and by the time of the Warring States was already at a flourishing, well-developed stage. Lacquered objects of this period were used very extensively, as containers for food and drink, as articles of daily use, as stationery, musical instruments and even weapons, means of transportation and funerary objects. The body of a lacquered object was made of wood, bamboo or hide and sometimes reinforced with ramie. Very often designs were carved on it, turning it into an exquisite work of art. The techniques for decorating lacquered objects were well developed during the Warring States Period. The designs were vividly and beautifully executed in a rich variety of colors; some reflected reality, others had a strong aura of mystery.

Spinning and Weaving, Tanning, Ceramics, Glazing, Jade Carving, Gold and Silver Work

Handicrafts such as spinning and weaving, tanning, ceramics, glazing, jade carving, gold and silver work all saw new progress during the Warring States Period. Quality items were produced in nearly all the states.

29. Fragments of woven fabric Chu relics, Warring States Period; unearthed at Wulipai and Xujiawan, Changsha City, Hunan Province, in 1951-52. Fragments of woven material unearthed at these two places included pieces *of juan* (tough, thin silk), silk, silk-woven nets, silk and cotton quilts, linen, embroidery, brocade sash and fine gauze. Chu had a highly developed silk-weaving industry. Nearly all of the earliest and best-preserved silk products discovered to date in China are of Chu origin. Important examples are the objects recovered from the Chu tombs at Mashan and Wangshan in Hubei Province, at Changtaiguan, Xinyang, in Henan Province, and at Zuojiatang, Changsha, and Guangjiqiao in Hunan Province. They included pieces of brocade, silk, thick silk, silk ribbons, gauze, *zu* and damask in a variety of colors: red, yellow, green, blue, purple and brown. Both the dyeing and the embroidery were superb, evidence of the remarkably high level of dyeing and weaving techniques in ancient China.

30

30. Porcelain pot with dragon handle
Chu wine container, Warring States Period, height 18 cm, mouth diameter 7 cm; unearthed at Lizhu, Shaoxing, Zhejiang Province, in 1955. This pot is made of very hard clay mixed with sand and surfaced with a thin layer of glaze. It has a round mouth, sloping shoulders, a protruding belly and a dragon-shaped loop handle. The back of the dragon is serrated like the teeth of a saw. Its head is a part of the spout. The three legs of the pot are like hooves. The belly and the upper part of the lid are ornamented with fingernail patterns. It is a good example of China's early primitive green porcelain, predecessor of the green porcelain that matured during the Han Dynasty. Han green porcelain articles were produced mainly in Shangyu and Shaoxing in what is now Zhejiang Province. But kilns for firing primitive green porcelain dating back to the Warring States Period have also been discovered near Shaoxing, evidence that the green porcelains of the two periods were closely related in their origins.

31. Silver belt fastener with gold plating, jade inlay, and glazed pearls Wei relic, Warring States Period, 18.4 cm long, 4.9 cm wide; unearthed from Tomb 1, Guwei Village, Hui County, Henan Province, in 1951. This belt fastener is made of silver and plated with gold. It was cast with relief images of animal heads and long-tailed birds. The animal heads occupied the two ends of the fastener while the birds sat or coiled on the sides. Three pieces of white jade were inlaid into the upper surface of the fastener, and a glazed pearl was set in the center of each piece like the eye of a dragonfly. The hook at the front end of the fastener is also made of white jade and is shaped like the head of a wild goose. Tomb 1 at Guwei Village, Hui County, was the burial place of a great nobleman of Wei, a powerful state of the mid-Warring States Period. It had occupied parts of Qin territory west of the Yellow River, conquered Zhongshan state, severely defeated Qi, captured the Chu city of Daliang (present-day Kaifeng, Henan) and moved its capital there.

31

32. Green jade pendant with cloud-and-animal design Wei ornament, Warring States Period, 20.5 cm long, 4.8 cm wide; unearthed from Tomb l, Guwei Village, Hui County, Henan Province, in 1951. This pendant is composed of seven pieces of jade openwork, joined by copper plates into a semi-annular ornament. Above the middle piece is an image of a crouching horse, and below it is a small ring. The whole object is decorated with dragon images and a variant cloud pattern. The exposed parts of the copper are shaped like ogre masks plated with gold. Although primarily for decorative purposes, jade pendants were also used as ritual objects in court ceremonies and during sacrifices and funerals. A pendant as elaborate as this one, however, is rare.

33

33. Opaque colored glass ball   Ornament of the Warring States Period, vertical diameter 6.3 cm, horizontal diameter 6.2 cm. It is made of glaze (primitive glass) inlaid with colored material. The background is purple and decorated with opaque light blue pearls resembling the eyes of dragonflies. Opaque glass balls inlaid with colored material have been found in large quantities in China, Southeast Asia, West Asia, and along the eastern coast of the Mediterranean. Although found in different places, the balls are very similar in form and color, evidence of the development and interchange of glassware in these regions. Glass balls as large as this one are rare.

34. Jade pendants   Ornaments worn on the body, Zeng relics, Warring States Period, 10.3 cm long, 2.4 cm wide, 0.3 cm thick; unearthed from Tomb 1 at Leigudun, Sui County, Hubei Province, in 1978. These two pendants are green and white in color, and are long, narrow and slightly curved. Small holes were bored in the center and at the two ends of each pendant, both sides of which were decorated with grain patterns. In addition to numerous large-sized bronzes and

bamboo and wooden articles, a total of 528 ornaments made of jade, stone, crystal, amethyst and glass were found in the tomb, mostly in the inner coffin, suggesting that most of these funerary objects were the personal property of the grave occupant when he or she was alive. There was a superstition in ancient times that burying jade objects with a corpse could prevent it from decaying, which presumably is one reason why so many jade ornaments were buried in the tomb.

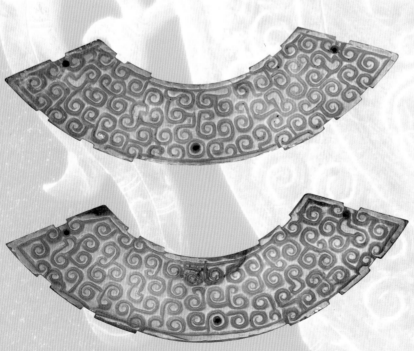

34

35

35. Ganyou silver ladle Relic of the Warring States Period, Eastern Zhou, height 3.7 cm, mouth length 11 cm, width 9.8 cm; said to have been unearthed at Jin Village, Luoyang City, Henan Province. The ladle is made of pure silver. Two characters that read "ganyou" in *pinyin* transliteration are inscribed on the bottom; they are probably the name of a palace building. This gourd-shaped ladle is the earliest piece of silverware discovered in China. Jin Village was a cemetery of the Eastern Zhou royal family, and this ladle may have been a utensil in the royal household. Large feudal states were fighting for supremacy at this time and the Zhou king was merely the titular ruler of the country. He ruled symbolically from a corner of Luoyang, and had as much power as a minor feudal lord. He was deposed when Qin overthrew the Zhou Dynasty in the last years of the Warring States Period.

Cities and Commerce

A large number of cities were built during the Warring States Period. The most highly developed commercial cities were Linzi, Handan, Ji and Wan. By the mid-Warring States Period, to meet the growing needs of trade, the various states began minting large quantities of coins and setting up their own systems of weights and measures.

36

36. Half of an eaves tile with ogre mask Yan building material, Warring States Period, 9.8 cm high, 19.8 cm in diameter; unearthed from the ruins of the Yan capital, Xiadu, in Yi County, Hebei Province, in 1930. This eaves tile, which bears a solemn and fierce-looking ogre mask, was used on the roof of the Yan royal palace. Xiadu was built during the reign of King Zhao of Yan. It stood at a key point on the road to the states of Qi and Zhao and was an important political, economic and military stronghold of southern Yan. Excavations conducted there since 1930 have uncovered the remains of many buildings, large and small, all part of palace complexes. Among the relics were animal-shaped clay pipes and beautifully decorated tiles and half-tiles, discoveries that afford valuable first-hand material for the study of the scale, layout and decorative art of urban construction in ancient Yan.

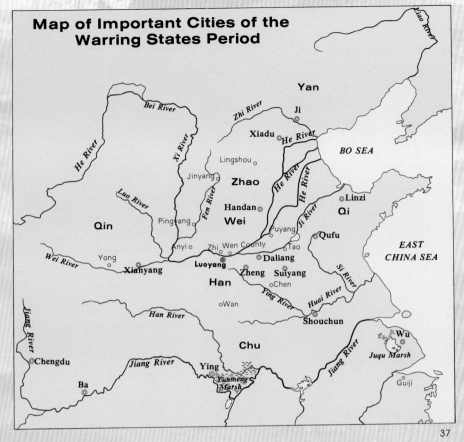

Map of Important Cities of the Warring States Period

(map labels)

Liao River

Yan

Bei River

Zhi River

Ji

He River

Xiadu

He River

Xi River

Lingshou

BO SEA

He River

Jinyang

Zhao

Fen River

Luo River

Handan

Linzi

Qin

Pingyang

Wei

Ji River

Qi

Anyi

Zhi Wen County

Puyang

Qufu

Wei River

Yong

Luoyang

Tao

EAST CHINA SEA

Xianyang

Daliang

Si River

Zheng

Suiyang

Han

oChen

Jiang River

oWan

Ying River

Huai River

Han River

Shouchun

Chengdu

Chu

Wu

Jiang River

Juqu Marsh

Jiang River

Ba

Ying

Yunmeng Marsh

Guiji

37

37. Map of important cities of the Warring States Period

"Cities 1,000 *zhang* square with 10,000 households gaze at one another" [a *zhang* is roughly three meters]. This saying reflects the existence of many large cities during the Warring States Period. Among the richest and most populous cities were the capitals of the larger feudal states such as Ying (now Jinan, north of Jingshan, Hubei), capital of Chu; Xianyang (now Xianyang, Shaanxi), capital of Qin; Handan (now Handan, Hebei), capital of Zhao; Daliang (now Kaifeng, Henan), capital of Wei; Xinzheng (now Xinzheng County, Henan), capital of Han; Ji (southwest of Beijing), capital of Yan; Linzi (north of Zibo, Shandong), capital of Qi; and the cities Zhuo (now Zhuozhou, Hebei) of Yan; Wen (southwest of Wen County, Henan) and Zhi (southeast of Jiyuan County, Henan) of Wei; Xingyang (northeast of Xingyang County, Henan) of Han; Wan (now Yuzhou, Henan) and Chen (now Huaiyang, Henan) of Chu; Yangzhai (now Nanyang, Henan) of

Zheng; and Erzhou (now Luoyang, Henan) of Sanchuan. Additionally, Jimo (southeast of Pingdu, Shandong) and Xue (southeast of Teng County, Shandong) of Qi; Ling (west of Lishi County, Shanxi) and Lishi (now Lishi County, Shanxi) of Zhao; Anyi (northwest of Xia County, Shanxi) of Wei; Zhangzi (southwest of Zhangzi County, Shanxi) and Tunliu (south of Tunliu County, Shanxi) of

Han; Shouchun (now Shou County, Anhui) of Chu; and Yong (now Fengxiang County, Shaanxi) of Qin were also large and prosperous cities.

38. Semicylindrical tiles with *fufu* patterns

Yan building material, Warring States Period, length 90.2 cm, diameter 36 cm; said to have been unearthed from the ruins of the ancient Yan city of Xiadu in Yi County, Hebei Province. The body of the tile is impressed with imitation triangular *fufu* (patterns used to embroider ceremonial robes in ancient times) which were arranged in two groups. Tiles like this were probably laid along the top of palace walls as a protective covering. Ancient Xiadu was eight kilometers long from east to west and four kilometers wide from north to south. A waterway running north to south across the center of the city divided it into an east city and a west city. The east city was also called the inner city. The northern part of this inner city, where the Central Wuyang Terrace and Laolao Terrace were located, was the palace district. To judge from the large well-made cylintrical tiles with *fufu* patterns unearthed there, the palaces of Xiadu must have been magnificent buildings.

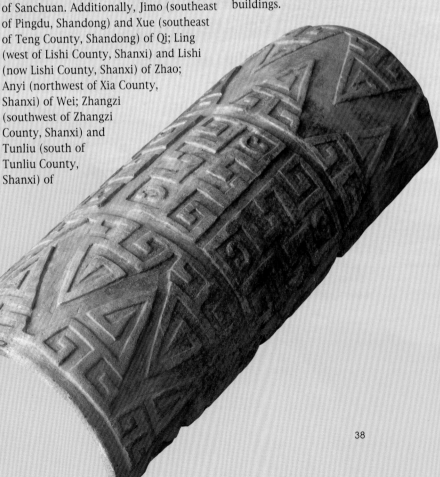

38

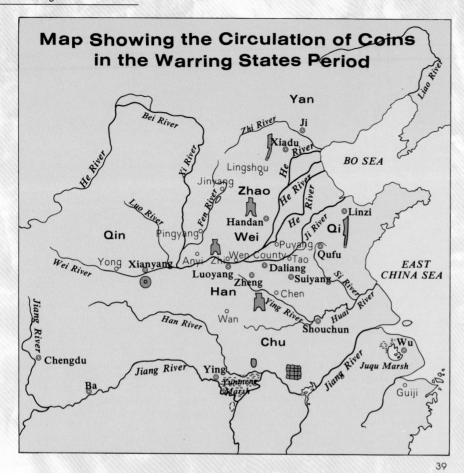

Map Showing the Circulation of Coins in the Warring States Period

39

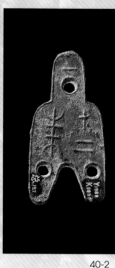

40-1   40-2

39. Map showing the circulation of coins in the Warring States Period Bronze coins and gold were the chief currencies of the Warring States Period. Bronze currencies were of the following kinds: *bu* (cloth), *dao* (knife-shaped), *yuan* (round) and *bei* (shell) [*bu* and *bei* coins were not actually made of cloth and shell]. *Bu* coins were circulated mainly in the states of Han, Zhao and Wei (collectively called the "Three Jin" district). *Dao* currency was used chiefly in the states of Qi, Yan and Zhao. *Yuan* currency was used mainly in East and West Zhou and in the territories of Zhao and Wei along the Yellow River. *Bei* currency was use mainly in Chu. Gold currency was also circulated mainly in Chu, and was of two kinds, coins and blocks. Most gold blocks bore stamped imprints, some of which read, in *pinyin* transliteration: *yingcheng, chencheng, tuancheng, ying, qinjin.*

40. Three-hole *bu* coin of Songzi Zhao currency, Warring States Period, 5.4 cm long, 2.8 cm wide; unearthed in Pingshuo County, Shanxi Province. The coin had two circular legs with a hole in each and a third hole at the top. On the coin are two characters that read in *pinyin* transliteration "Songzi," the place where the coin was minted. On the back is the inscription "12 zhu," the weight of the coin. One *zhu* was roughly .04 catty.

41. Three-Jin *bu* coins Currency of the Warring States Period. Such coins were used mainly in the three states of Han, Zhao and Wei, known as the Three-Jin district. These variously shaped coins are collectively called Three-Jin *bu* coins. From left to right in photo: **Lishi round-leg *bu* coin:** This was a Zhao coin. It has a flat top, round shoulders and round legs,

and is 7.2 cm high, 3.1 cm wide at the shoulders and 3.8 cm wide at the base. It was minted at Lishi (now Lishi County, Shanxi).   **Jinyang *bu* coin with pointed legs:** This is a coin with a flat top, raised shoulders and pointed legs, 8.2 cm high, 3.8 cm wide at the shoulders and 4.5 cm wide at the base. It was used in Zhao during the early years of the Warring States Period. It was minted in Jinyang (modern Taiyuan, Shanxi). **Liang chong jin, 50 to 1 *lue*:** This was a Wei coin. It has round shoulders, a bridgelike crotch and square legs, and is 6 cm high, 3.6 cm wide at the shoulders and 3.8 cm wide at the base. The word *liang* inscribed on the coin referred to Daliang, Wei's capital. All *bu* coins bearing this word were minted after Wei moved its capital there. *Chong* means the same as *zhong* (weight). *Jin* and *lue* were ancient units of weight. *Lue* was used to measure the weight of gold; its equivalent in other units of weight is not known. The term "50 to 1 *lue* " means that 50 pieces of the coin was equal in value to one *lue* of gold.

42. *Dao* coins of Qi Currency of the Warring States Period; left to right: **Qi jianbangchang:** 18.2 cm long, 2.95 cm wide; used in Qi during the late Warring States Period. It is an attractive and well-made coin and bears the longest inscription of all knife-shaped coins of Qi, but not very many pieces of it are extant.

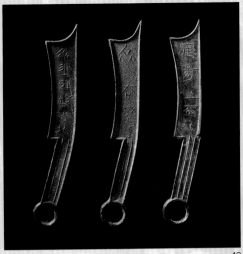

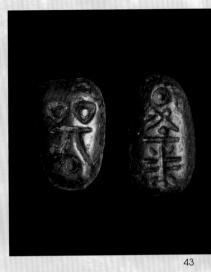

41

42

43

Qi *baohuo*: 18.7 cm long, 3 cm wide. Knife-shaped Qi coins are relatively large in size. The inscriptions on them usually give the name of the place where they were made and the name of the currency, *baohuo*. There are usually three horizontal lines, a nail-like pattern and a single character on the back of the coin. On the one shown here the character is the Chinese word for sun. ***Baohuo* of Anyang:** 18.5 cm long, 2.9 cm wide. Anyang was where this coin was minted. It is near Ju County in Shandong Province. On the back of most Anyang *baohuo* coins are three horizontal lines with an inscription below. The inscription on the coin shown here reads "huo" in *pinyin* transliteration.

43. Bronze *bei* coins Chu currency, Warring States Period; unearthed in Shou County, Anhui Province. The one on the left is 1.7 cm long and 1.2 cm wide; the one on the right, 1.9 cm long and 1.1 cm wide. Bronze *bei* coins were imitations of ancient shell money with the back of the shell rubbed smooth. On the surface of such coins are incised characters such as 哭、俗、金、行、君. The character most frequently seen was 𩇩. Such coins were popularly called "ghost-face money" or "ant-nose money." They were widely distributed and used for a relatively long time in Chu.

44. *Yingcheng* and *lujin* Chu currencies, Warring States Period; unearthed at Huayuancun, Dongjin Village, Shou County, Anhui Province, in 1979. The *yingcheng* is 7 cm long and 7.3 cm wide; the *lujin*, 9.3 cm long and 7 cm wide. These coins were made of pure gold. They are flat pieces shaped like plates and are stamped with Chinese characters. The character for *cheng* on the *yingcheng* coin was a unit of weight; *ying* was a place name. Other similar coins used in Chu were the *chencheng* and *tuancheng*. The *lujin* had a circular seal on it with the Chinese characters for *lujin*. *Lu* was also a place name. The *yingcheng* and *lujin* were China's earliest gold money. When used they were cut into small pieces, which were valued according to their weight.

44

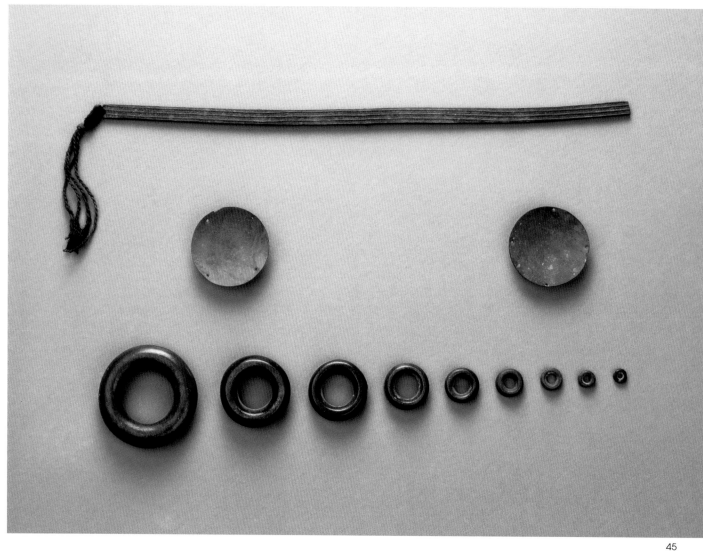

45

45. Scale and ring weights Chu weighing apparatus, Warring States Period; unearthed at Zuojiagongshan, Changsha, Hunan Province, in 1954. The scale consisted of a horizontal wooden beam and two bronze pans. The beam was a flat piece 27 cm long with a hole in the middle, through which a silk cord was passed serving as a suspender. Each pan was 4 cm in diameter, with four symmetrically spaced holes along the rim. Silk threads were passed through the holes, by means of which the pans were hung to the two ends of the beam. The weights of the nine rings, from small to large, were 0.6 g, 1.2 g, 2.1 g, 4.6 g, 8 g, 15.6 g, 31.3 g, 61.82 g, 125 g. This ancient scale with a complete set of weights was a very rare discovery. According to tests made, the weights of the rings, in terms of the units used at the time, were 1 *zhu*, 2 *zhu*, 3 *zhu*, 6 *zhu*, 12 *zhu*, 1 *liang*, 2 *liang*, 4 *liang*, 8 liang respectively (one *zhu* was 1/24 of a *liang*). A Chu catty (16 *liang*) was approximately 250 grams. Chu was commercially well developed and its weights and measures were fairly accurate and standardized. The kinds of currency used in Chu were the bronze *bei* and gold blocks. Presumably this small scale was used to weigh pieces cut from a gold block.

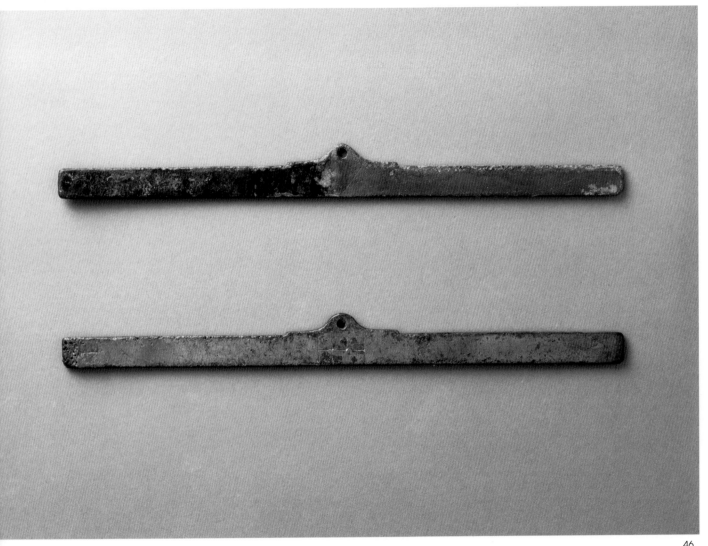

46

46. Bronze scales with Chinese character for "king" Chu weighing scales, Warring States Period; said to have been unearthed in Shou County, Anhui Province. These two scales were similar in form and make-up. Both were long flat bars with the Chinese character for "king" inscribed on the upper side. One was 23.1 cm long, 1 cm wide, 0.35 cm thick; the other, 23.15 cm long, 1.3 cm wide, 0.35 cm thick. At the center, or fulcrum, was a protuberance with a hole, through which a string was looped for lifting the scale. The length of these scales was the equivalent of one *chi* (foot) in the Warring States Period. They were graduated with lines cut into the front side. On one scale the lines divided it into ten equal parts each one *cun* (inch) long. On the other, the two parts in the center adjacent to the fulcrum were one inch long, but all the other parts were only half an inch. The distance from the weight to the fulcrum and from the weighed object to the fulcrum were measured by these lines. The weight of an object was calculated from these measurements. These scales were fairly accurate measuring instruments. The character for "king" was probably an indication that the devices belonged to the Chu royal family.

Science, Culture, Contention of a Hundred Schools

Establishment of the feudal system, economic growth, and intensified wars for unification led to the development of science and culture and to great activity on the academic and ideological fronts. New breakthroughs in science and culture pushed many disciplines to the advanced world levels of their time. They also helped to elucidate and promote many profound philosophical theories, thus enriching the ideological treasure-house of ancient China.

Contention of a Hundred Schools

The days when learning was the monopoly of feudal officials were over. Private schools were set up all over the country, and supporting and helping learned men became a vogue. Representatives of different schools wrote books, put forward theories, discussed politics, expounded philosophical principles, debated, argued, and tried to influence each other. It was a situation of "a hundred schools of thought contending."

48

Principal Schools of the Warring States Period

School	Chief Representative (s)
Mohists	Mo Di
Confucianists	Meng Ke, Xun Kuang
Taoists	Zhuang Zhou
Legalists	Li Kui, Shang Yang, Han Fei
Logicians	Hui Shi, Gongsun Long
Yin-Yang	Zhou Yan
Political Strategists	Zhang Yi, Sun Qin
Military Strategists	Sun Bin, Wu Qi
Agriculturists	Xu Xing
Eclectics	Lü Buwei

像 子 莊

47. Portrait of Zhuang Zhou

Zhuang Zhou (c.369-280 BC) was a native of Meng (northeast of present-day Shangqiu, Henan) of the state of Song during the Warring States Period. He was a noted thinker of the Taoist school. He believed that "Taoist laws followed nature," that *tao* (sometimes translated as "the way") was unlimited; that it transcended time and space and could not be felt or understood; that it gave birth to all living creatures but had its own root and origin that could not be fathomed. He held that the ultimate in learning *tao* was to eliminate all differences. So he advocated a passive nonaction and absolute spiritual freedom. In his methods of thinking and argument, he showed a tendency to mystify relativity and render it absolute.

47

49

48. Portrait of Meng Ke Meng Ke
(c.372—289 BC), styled Ziyu, also known
as Mencius, was a native of Zou (southeast
of modern Zou County, Shandong). He
was a famous thinker of the Confucian
school of the Warring States Period,
representing orthodox Confucianism. He
preached learning from the earlier kings,
"benevolent government," "protecting the
people is the kingly way" and "union is
stability." He put forward the slogan that
"the people are great but the monarch is
small" and called for improvement of
relations between the ruler and the ruled.
Proceeding from the premise that "all
humans are born good," he stressed
cultivation of the individual's mind and
character. His most important work is
Mencius, in seven chapters, written late in
life with the help of his disciples Wan
Zhang and Gongsun Chou.

49. Portrait of Xun Kuang Xun Kuang
(c.313—238 BC), also called Xunzi, native
of Zhao, was a famous thinker of the late
Warring States Period. His thinking
originated in the Confucian school but
also absorbed the theories of the Legalists
and Taoists. In his view of natural laws, he
argued that "man and heaven should be
separated" and that "heaven's laws can be
controlled and utilized." In epistemology,
his theory was that "action is more
important than knowledge." Regarding
human nature, he held that "humans were
born evil." In politics, he advocated
"learning from the later kings" (Kings
Wen and Wu and Regent Zhou Gong of the
Western Zhou) and "using grand rituals to
enforce the law" so as to realize the
"kingly way." In particular, he stressed
the role of rites in "transforming nature,"
which had a profound influence on latter-
day Confucianists.

**50. *Lü's Spring and Autumn Annals*,
Ming edition** This book was compiled by

Lü Buwei, prime minister of Qin, and his
house guests. It was completed on the eve
of Qin's unification of China and
contained a text of over 200,000 words in
26 volumes, of which 12 were historical
records, 8 were readings, and 6 were
dissertations. The basic thread of thought
was Taoism, but the best of other schools
such as Confucianism, Mohism, Legalism
and the School of Military Strategists were
also included. The purpose was to present
the best of different schools, summarize
historical experiences, and provide a
program for governing the country under
an autocratic central power that was to
be established after unification.
Preserving many old sayings and
anecdotes, the book is valued both
for its theoretical expositions
and the abundant historical
materials it provides.

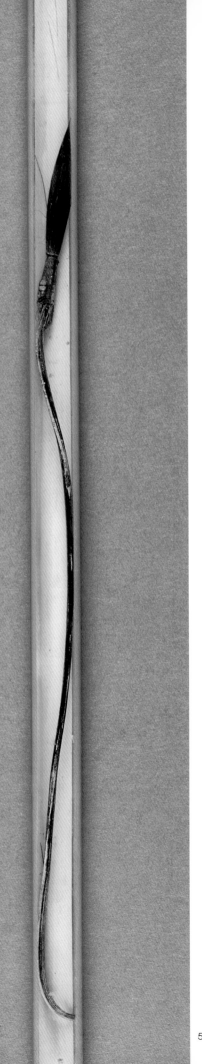

Art, Culture and the Natural Sciences

New achievements were recorded in such disciplines as astronomy, optics, geoscience and agronomy. *Astronomy and Astrology* by Gan De of Qi and *Astronomy* by Shi Shen of Wei (two books often referred to as the *Gan-Shi Classic of the Stars*) each listed the celestial longitudes and latitudes of 800 stars. They were the earliest star catalogues in the world, antedating by some 200 years the first European one, compiled by Hipparchus in 129 BC.*Yu Gong*, or *Yu's Book of Geography*, was completed during the Warring States Period. Covering the mountains, rivers, soil, land taxes, mineral resources, flora and fauna, and national minorities in all nine divisions of ancient China, it is the first systematic treatise on Chinese geography. *Mo Jing* (a book compiled by latter-day adherents of the Mocian school) is one of the earliest treatises on geometrical optics in the world. Among other things it observed and studied the images formed by pinholes and by plane, concave and convex mirrors; and put forward the theory that light travels in a straight line. *Xia Xiaozheng*, one of the oldest extant works on phenology, records month by month the natural phenomena and farm activities of its time. The methods of diagnosis—watching, listening, asking, feeling the pulse—put forward by Qin Yueren (a folk doctor better known as Bian Que) and the *Classic of Internal Medicine* are summaries based on practice of theories concerning the internal organs and channels of the human body and the causes of disease. An overview of Chinese medical experiences down to the Qin-Han era, they laid the theoretical foundation of Chinese medicine.

Important achievements were also made in the realms of literature, history, painting, and song and dance. Prose writings by scholars of the Warring States Period laid the foundation for the development of Chinese prose. Qu Yuan's *Chu Ci* (*The Songs of Chu*) opened the path for the development of Chinese romanticist lyric poetry. *Zuo Zhuan* (*Zuo's Commentary on the Spring and Autumn Annals*) and *Guo Yu* (*Sayings of the States*) contributed fundamentally to the compilation of chronological and national histories.

51. Brush pen Chu writing implement, Warring States Period; unearthed at Zuojiagongshan, Changsha, Hunan Province, in 1954. When discovered, it was encased in a bamboo tube 23.2 cm long. The brush itself was 21.2 cm long with a cylindrical handle of solid bamboo and a tuft of rabbit hair. One end of the handle was split into several parts, and the tuft was inserted in between them. The parts were then bound together with a silk thread and varnished to keep them in place. Writing brushes have been used in China for thousands of years, beginning no later than the Shang Dynasty. However, because they rotted easily, relics of such brushes are hard to find. The one shown here is the oldest brush discovered to date.

53

54

52. *Lingshu.Suwen*, Ming edition   This is the earliest systematic treatise on medicine in Chinese history. The two parts, *Lingshu* (*Miraculous Pivot*) and *Suwen* (*Plain Questions*), together are called *The Yellow Emperor's Classic of Internal Medicine*, but it is quite certain that this comprehensive treatise was not the work of one man. More likely it was compiled by some school of the Warring States Period and took many years to complete. On the basis of centuries of medical practice, it summed up and put forward theories concerning the viscera and channels and the causes of disease, establishing the theoretical basis of traditional Chinese medicine. It is a summary of medical experiences before the Qin-Han dynasties. The medical theories contained in the two parts complement each other, but *Linshu* discusses mainly the channels and acupuncture points of the human body and methods of acupuncture. Therefore, later generations called it the *Classic of Acupuncture*. *Suwen* uses chiefly the theories of *yin-yang* to expound human physiology, pathology and the causes of disease, stressing that to cure a disease one must find its root cause, then make an overall analysis on the basis of the cause and form of the disease and the affected parts of the body. Its guiding principle was to "dispel pathogenic factors to restore the normal functions of the body." This is the basic theory of traditional Chinese medicine.

53. Portrait of Qu Yuan   Qu Yuan (c.339—278 BC) was a famous statesman and man of letters of Chu. He served for a time as the *zuotu* (assistant prime minister) of King Huai of Chu. His policy was to build an honest and enlightened government and enter into an alliance with Qi to resist Qin. But because he infringed upon the interests of the Chu nobility, he was libeled and lost the favor of the king. Later, in the reign of King Xiang, he was exiled to south of the Yangtze. During his estrangement and exile he composed many poems revealing his love and longing for his homeland and his sorrow over the times. In 278 BC, when Qin captured Chu's capital Ying (now Jinan City, north of Jingsha, Hubei), the poet overwhelmed with grief and despair drowned himself in the Miluo River (in Miluo County, Hunan). His important works included *Li Sao* (*Lament*), *Jiuzhang* (*Nine Chapters*), *Tianwen* (*Asking Heaven*) and *Jiuge* (*Nine Songs*).

54. *Poems of Chu*, Ming edition   This is a collection of long poems by Qu Yuan (it includes a few by Song Yu, Jing Cha, Tang Le and others). It is divided into the following parts: "Lament," "Nine Chapters," "Recalling the Soul," "Nine Songs" and "Asking Heaven." Most of them were laments about worldly sorrows and the troubled times. They were originally composed in a Chu dialect prevalent in the region of the Yangtze and Han rivers. Inheriting traditional styles and absorbing the essence of songs and poems of the Central Plains, Qu Yuan rewrote those Chu poems, improved on them, and turned them into long lyrics rich in imagination and romanticism. His writings represented a big leap forward in the history of Chinese poetry. Using numerous myths and legends, those Chu poems reflected the poet's longing for his homeland and his thoughts and feelings in the struggle against decadent forces in society. His patriotism is revealed most strongly in "Lament," "Nine Chapters" and "Recalling the Soul." "Asking Heaven" poses over 170 questions covering a wide and varied field, from the origins of the universe to its composition, from myths and legends to the era of history. The writings reveal the profundity of the poet's thinking and his penetrating insight. "Nine Songs" consists of revised and adapted versions of folk songs of southern Chu, sung during sacrifices to the gods. They represent a certain aspect of the shamanistic culture of southern Chu.

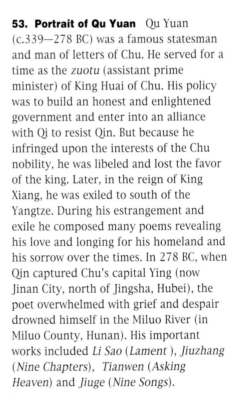

55. Bronze chimes Chu musical instrument, Warring States Period; unearthed at Changtaiguan, Xinyang, Henan Province, in 1957. This is a set of 13 bells hung on a rack by means of 13 sheathlike hooks. The heights of the bells, in the order of their size, are 30.5 cm, 25.7 cm, 24.5 cm, 23.4 cm, 21.8 cm, 21.4 cm, 20.3 cm, 19 cm, 17.6 cm, 16.6 cm, 15.9 cm, 15.5 cm and 13 cm. Cast on the two sides of the first or largest bell are 12 characters recording how Jing Li of Chu repulsed an attack by the armies of Jin and saved the Rong people living in Chu. The bells were accurately tuned and produced melodious sounds.

55-2

56. Stone chimes Wei musical instrument, Warring States Period; unearthed at Houchuan, Shaan County, Henan Province, in 1957. This is a set of ten chimes whose lengths and widths, in the order of their size, are 72.9 and 17.7 cm, 66 and 16 cm, 48.7 and 14.5 cm, 48.1 and 15.5 cm, 48 and 15.2 cm, 41 and 13.5 cm, 38 and 12.5 cm, 32.6 and 11.25 cm, 30.6 and 11.1 cm, 29 and 10.3 cm. The chimes were hung upon a rack and struck to produce musical notes. The rack shown here is patterned on the one with bronze chimes unearthed at Changtaiguan, Xinyang, Henan Province. Tomb 2040 at Houchuan, Shaan County, in which this set of stone chimes was found, is a very large and elaborate tomb, from which a large number of relics have been recovered. Over 80 pieces have been counted, of one category of large-sized bronzes. Wei was a powerful state of the early Warring States Period and the set of stone chimes shown here suggests that the tomb occupant was a high-ranking official.

National Minorities of the Warring States Period

Relations between the feudal states and minority peoples living along their borders were continually strengthened during the Warring States Period. The Han and minority peoples influenced each other, merged, and in some cases the minorities were annexed through war.

Minorities in the North and Northeast

Among the minorities living in the northern and northeastern parts of the country during the Warring States Period were the Linhu, Loufan and Donghu tribes, nomads who settled wherever there was grass and water, and the Eastern Yi tribes whose main occupations were farming and stock raising.

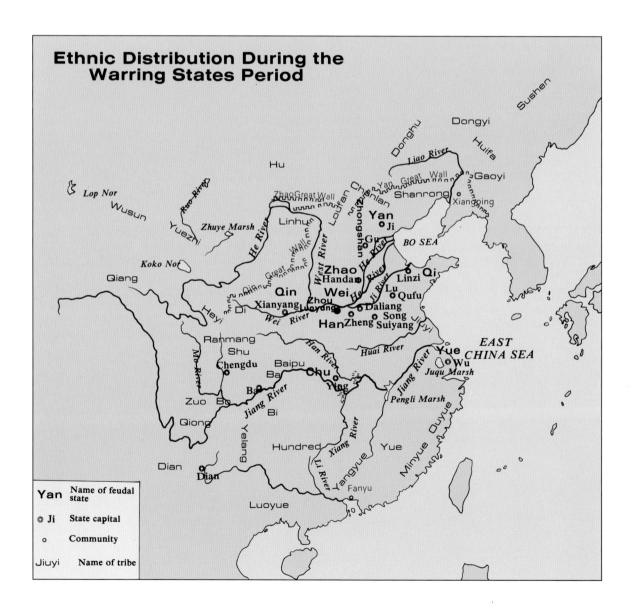

58

57

57. Bronze horse head ornament with frog-snake design Donghu relic, Warring States Period, 20 cm long, 5.7 cm wide; unearthed at Sanguan Dianzi, Lingyuan County, Liaoning Province, in 1976. This is an ornament for the head of a horse. It is a lively and realistic portrayal of a fat frog with protruding eyes, whose front legs rest on the ground and hind legs are in the mouths of two intertwining snakes. The Donghu (Eastern Hu) were a nomadic tribe that inhabited the upper reaches of the Liao River in western Liaoning Province during the Warring States Period. They were expert horsemen and archers, settled wherever there was grass and water, and had economic ties with the states of Yan and Zhao, whose territory they encroached upon from time to time. This horse head ornament reflects an aspect of their nomadic life.

58. Gold ornamental plate with design of tigers fighting bulls Hu ornament of the Warring States Period, 12.7 cm long, 7.4 cm wide, weight 237.625 g; unearthed at Aludeng, Hanggin Banner, Ih Ju League of the Inner Mongolia Autonomous Region, in 1972. This gold plate is impressed with a design of four tigers and bulls fighting each other. It is a vivid and realistic depiction of certain features of the environment in which the Hu people of the grasslands lived. The Linhu and Loufan (Hu tribes) who inhabited the Mongolian highlands to the north of Yan and Zhao were still living under a patriarchal slave system during the Warring States Period. They were good at riding and shooting, had some economic dealings with Yan and Zhao, and frequently invaded or harassed the Central Plains. The implements they used were in the artistic style of nomadic peoples but were also influenced by the culture of the Central Plains.

Yue Tribes of the South and Southeast

During the Warring States Period, Yue tribes inhabited what are now southern Jiangsu Province, Zhejiang Province, Fujian Province, Jiangxi Province, southern Hunan Province, Guangdong and Guangxi. Comprising numerous branches, they were collectively called the Baiyue (Hundred Yues), whose economic development was very uneven.

59. Shoe-shaped bronze battle-axe
Baiyue weapon, Warring States Period, height 8.5 cm, width of blade 13.7 cm; unearthed at Yinshanling, Pingle County, Guangxi Zhuang Autonomous Region, in 1974. Shaped like a leather boot, this weapon of the Baiyue (Hundred Yue) people is in a distinctive local style different from weapons used in the Central Plains in those days.

59

60. Square column-shaped bolts with human head images Baiyue relics, Warring States Period; unearthed in Sihui County, Guangdong Province, in 1973. One is 24.1 cm long, 2.3 cm wide and 2 cm thick, with a bolt 8.7 cm long at the bottom. The other is 23.5 cm long, 2.2 cm wide and 2 cm thick, with a bolt 8.2 cm long below. These bolts were probably used to secure the wooden parts of a coffin. The Baiyue (Hundred Yues) were tribes that inhabited areas south of Chu and Yue in the Warring States Period. The tribes that inhabited the southern part of Zhejiang Province and the region around modern Fuzhou in Fujian Province were called Minyue (Fujian Yue). Those inhabiting what are now Guangdong Province, the Guangxi Zhuang Autonomous Region and southern Jiangxi Province were called Nanyue (Southern Yue). During the last years of the Spring and Autumn Period, the Baiyue began merging with the Huaxia (Han Chinese) tribes of the Central Plains. By the time of the Warring States, their relations with the Central Plains had become very close. Baiyue bronzes had their own cultural features, an example of which is the figures of human heads carved at the end of the bolts shown here. But they also assimilated advanced ideas of the cultures of Chu and the Central Plains. These bolts are an example of the merging of Huaxia and Baiyue cultures.

60

Southwestern Minorities

Most of the minority peoples in the southwest boast long cultural traditions in their localities. Some, however, migrated from places in the northwest such as Gansu and Qinghai during the Warring States Period. The Shu and Ba peoples, in what is now Sichuan Province, assimilated much from the cultures of Qin and Chu, but the bronze culture of Yunnan and Guizhou possessed marked local characteristics.

61. Bronze *zheng* with image of tiger
Chu relic, Warring States Period, 39.3 cm long, 13.5 cm in diameter; said to have been unearthed in Xinjin County, Sichuan Province. A *zheng* was a bell-shaped percussion instrument used by an army on the march. This one has a fairly long handle. Carved on the front of the body are figures of a tiger and trees and an inscription in the Ba-Shu language, showing that it was an instrument used by the ancient Ba-Shu peoples. The Ba and Shu were tribes in what is now Sichuan Province. The Ba tribe inhabited the eastern part of the province; the Shu lived in western Sichuan in areas north of the upper reaches of the Yangtze. The latter had a well-developed agriculture during the late Spring and Autumn Period. They moved their capital to Chengdu during the mid-Warring States Period and became the head of the Rong-Di tribes in the region. Both the Ba and the Shu came under the influence of the cultures of Chu and Qin, but the figures of tigers, hands,

61-2

and base of flowers on their bronzeware were in their own tribal styles.

62. Bronze rhinoceros belt hook inlaid with gold and silver Ba relic, Warring States Period, 17.5 cm long, 6.5 cm high; unearthed at Baolunyuan, Zhaohua County, Sichuan Province, in 1954. The overall shape of this object is that of a one-horned rhinoceros with a double mane, a horn curled like a hook, and an elongated snout at the end of which is the figure of an animal's head. It is a most unusual shape. The Ba were an ancient tribe inhabiting the eastern part of Sichuan Province during the time of the Warring States. They used to hunt in boats on lakes and rivers; later they also engaged in farming. Their last capital was somewhere along the shores of the Jialing River near Chongqing. Because of their long-time proximity to Chu, they were profoundly influenced by Chu culture. Burying the dead in dugout canoes was a Ba custom.

Qin Dynasty

(221-206 BC)

In 221 BC, the state of Qin in the west finally conquered all six states in the east and established the first unified multiethnic country in Chinese history — the Qin Dynasty with its capital at Xianyang (now Xianyang City, Shaanxi Province). The

 Qin rulers set up a system of centralized state power and a system of prefectures and counties for the whole country. They consolidated the feudal system of land ownership, unified the country's written language and its weights and measures, built the Great Wall, and built orrepaired many roadways. In doing so, they established the basic political structure for all later feudal dynasties in China, as well as the basis for China's long-term unity. However, because of the tyranny of the First Emperor of Qin, his indiscriminate use of forced labor, and the weakness of his son and heir (called the Second Emperor), the outwardly powerful Qin Dynasty was overthrown in 206 BC, less than two decades after it was founded, by peasant armies with virtually no weapons.

Qin Conquers the Six States

Along with the development of the country's economy and culture, unification of the country became an irreversible trend in the late Warring States Period. During the ten years from 230 to 221 BC, King Ying Zheng of Qin annexed one by one the six states of Han, Zhao, Wei, Chu, Yan and Qi, ending a long period of divisive rule by feudal lords.

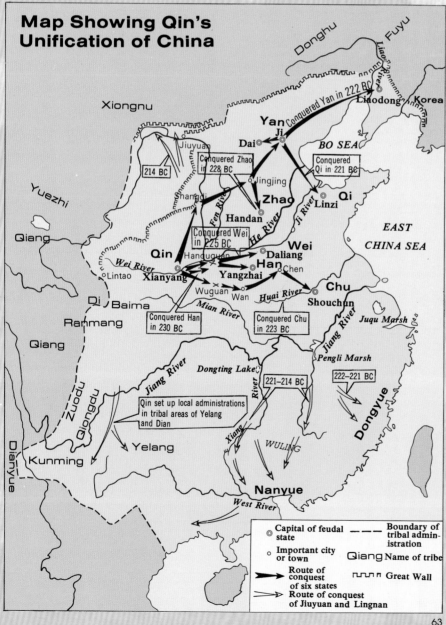

Map Showing Qin's Unification of China

63. Map of Qin's Unification of China

By the late Warring States Period the unification of the country had become an inevitable trend. King Zheng of Qin launched his final assault on the six other states by a strategy of allying himself with the more distant states and attacking those in his neighborhood. In 230 BC he made his first conquest, subduing his neighbor Han. In 228 BC, his general Wang Jian and others occupied Zhao; in 225 BC, Qin general Wang Bi reduced Wei; and in 223 BC, Wang Jian with an army 600,000 strong overran Chu. In 222 BC Wang Bi took Yan and the following year together with other Qin armies marched south and conquered the last enemy, Qi. Qin's conquest of the six states ended the era of divisive rule by feudal lords called the Warring States and ushered in a new era of feudal unity under the Qin and Han. Thereafter national unity was the mainstream in Chinese history.

64. *Annals* on bamboo slips Qin relic, unearthed in Yunmeng County, Hubei Province, in 1975. Altogether 53 slips were found, averaging 23.1-27.8 cm in length and 0.5-0.8 cm in width. They are also called *Records of Major Events*. A total of 550 characters have been counted, all written in ink in Qin seal script, and most of them are still clear and legible. There are no titles on any of the slips. The contents are mainly a year-by-year account of Qin's wars to unify the country and other major events from the first year (306 BC) of the Qin king Zhaoxiang's reign to the 33rd year (217 BC) of the First Emperor. Some of the material recorded on the slips accords with accepted history; some may be regarded as supplementary material. There are also parts that are like chronicles of personal histories. These *Annals* written on bamboo slips provide invaluable material on the military, political and calendrical systems of the Qin Dynasty; they are the oldest original historical writings extant.

65. Terra-cotta horse and warriors

Qin funerary objects, unearthed from the pits of the terra-cotta warriors in the First Emperor's mausoleum. One of the warriors is 188.57 cm tall, the other 190 cm. The horse is 215 cm long and 163 cm tall from hoof to top of head. Apart from pits l, 2 and 3 which have been uncovered successively since 1974, there is a fourth pit that was not completed. To judge from what has been discovered so far, the first three pits contained over 8,000 terra-cotta objects, which included about 130 war chariots, 500 chariot horses, 110 cavalry horses and 7,000 warriors. About 1,000 of these have been uncovered. Both men and horses were as large as life. These buried chariots, cavalry and foot soldiers represent in miniature the mighty army of Qin, with which the First Emperor conquered the six other states and unified the country as swiftly and easily as the autumn wind tosses fallen leaves.

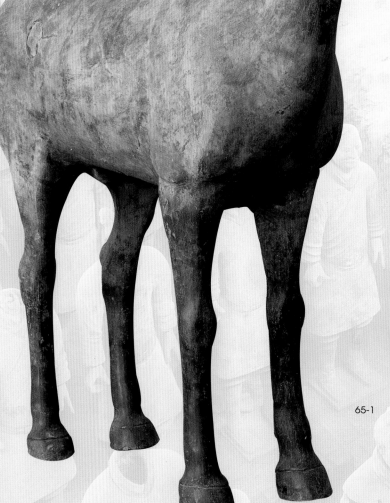

65-1

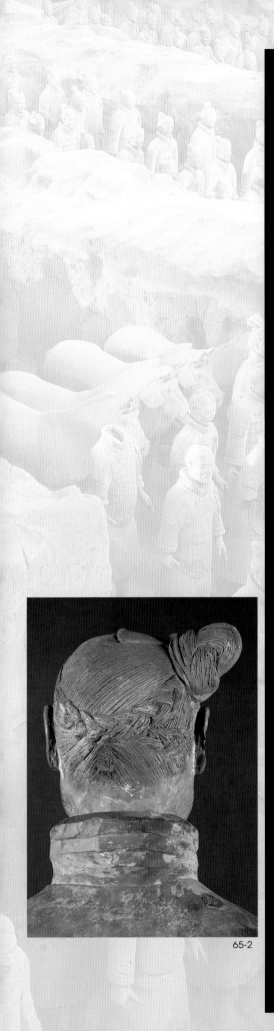

65-2

65-3

66. Bronze trigger mechanism of crossbow   Qin weapon, unearthed from one of the pits of the terra-cotta warriors in the First Emperor's mausoleum, Lintong, Shaanxi Province, in 1974. The bronze crossbow was a powerful weapon for shooting at distant targets. It first appeared in the early years of the Warring States. The bow on the earliest type of crossbow was drawn by hand and was called a thumb-drawn crossbow. Its effective range was only 80 meters. Later other types appeared, such as the foot-drawn crossbow and waist-drawn crossbow, both very powerful and deadly weapons. The trigger mechanism shown here belonged to an arm-drawn type. It consists of a tooth, a hook and a trigger. It does not have a metal case but is placed in a groove on the wooden stock of the bow, to which it is secured with pins. Like the other weapons unearthed from the pits of the terra-cotta warriors, it was used by the Qin army in its wars of conquest.

67. Bronze sword   Qin weapon, overall length 69 cm, weight 0.8 kg; unearthed from the Qin pits of terra-cotta warriors. The sword was a weapon for close combat. The swords of the Western Zhou and Spring and Autumn Period were relatively short and used mainly for self-defense. Those of the Warring States Period and the Qin Dynasty were longer and used by all infantry and cavalry troops.

66

67

68. Pottery figure: a groom Qin funerary object, 68 cm tall; unearthed in the area of the First Emperor's mausoleum, Lintong, Shaanxi Province. In recent years two pits containing real horses buried alive as funerary objects have been discovered on the grounds of the First Emperor's mausoleum. Clay figures, jars and basins were unearthed from the same pits. The jars and basins bore the names of five kinds of imperial stables: palace stable, central stable, large stable, left stable and third stable. We may infer from these names that the pits symbolized imperial stable grounds, the buried horses were imperial steeds, and the pottery figures were grooms.

68

Establishment of a Unified Country with Centralized State Power

After conquering the six other states, the king of Qin styled himself "emperor" and established an autocratic state with centralized power, administered through a system of prefectures and counties. To further consolidate the country's unity, he ordered the unification of the written language, currency, and weights and measures; built or repaired many roads; and built the Great Wall as a defensive barrier in the north.

Administrative Structure of the Qin Dynasty

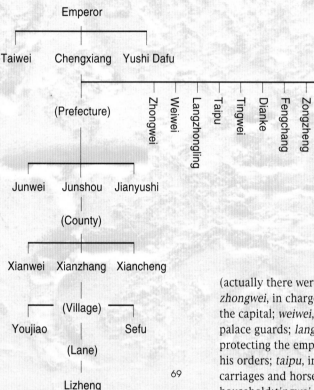

70

69. Centralized state power and system of prefectures and counties The king of Qin, after conquering the six other states, proclaimed himself the "first emperor," implying that there had been no real emperor before him. To strengthen the centralization of power, he set up a strict governmental structure and a bureaucratic system extending from the central government to the local levels. The central government directly under the emperor was headed by three officials of the highest rank called the *sangong* ("three seniors"): *chengxiang* (prime minister), *taiwei* (marshal) and *yushi dafu* (censor). The *chengxiang* assisted the emperor in administering political affairs; the *taiwei* was in charge of military affairs; and the *yushi dafu* was the chief censor. Under the *sangong* were nine ministers

(actually there were more than nine): *zhongwei*, in charge of public security in the capital; *weiwei*, the captain of the palace guards; *langzhongling*, in charge of protecting the emperor and transmitting his orders; *taipu*, in charge of the carriages and horses of the imperial household; *tingwei*, in charge of the judiciary and the administering of punishments; *dianke*, in charge of national minority and external affairs; *fengchang*, in charge of ancestral temples, ceremony and propriety; *zongzheng*, in charge of matters relating to the imperial family; *shaofu*, in charge of taxes on hills, seas, ponds and marshes and the handicrafts of local governments; *zhisu neishi*, in charge of tax revenue and expenditures. In the provinces a system of prefectures and counties was established. A prefecture was headed by a *junshou* (prefect), *junwei* and *jianyushi*, who were in charge of the prefecture's political, military and censorial affairs respectively. A county was headed by a *xianzhang* (magistrate), *xianwei* and *xiancheng*, who were also in charge of political, military and censorial matters respectively. Under the county were villages and lanes, units

responsible for educational matters, the collecting of taxes, corvée and maintenance of local order. All the chief officials from the central to the prefectural and county level were appointed and removed by order of the emperor; they received salaries but had no hereditary rights.

70. Portrait of the First Emperor of Qin The First Emperor of Qin (259—210 BC) was the founder of the Qin Dynasty. His family name was Ying and his first name Zheng. He became king of Qin at age 13 and began to rule on his own at age 22. In the ten years from 230 to 221 BC he conquered the six states of Han, Zhao, Wei, Chu, Yan and Qi and established the

first unified feudal state with centralized power in Chinese history. He styled himself the First Emperor, set up an administrative system of prefectures and counties over the country, and unified laws, weights and measures, the written language and currency. He sent troops north to fight the Xiongnu, built the Great Wall, subdued the Baiyue in the south, and developed both land and water transportation. These measures helped to consolidate the country's unity and promoted the development of the national economy and culture. But he ruled despotically, enacted harsh laws and punishments, levied heavy taxes and waged incessant wars, causing misery and suffering to the people and fomenting widespread discontent. Thus it was not long before the first great peasant uprising in Chinese history broke out.

71. Plate with edicts of First and Second Emperors of Qin Engraved in small seal script upon this bronze plate were the imperial edicts of Qin emperors on the unifying of the country's weights and measures. What still remains of the plate is 11.5 cm high and 13.4 cm wide. In 221 BC the First Emperor ordered his prime ministers Wei Zhuang and Wang Guan to promulgate for enforcement throughout the land the weights and measures of Qin which thereafter were to be the only lawful weights and measures. His 40-character edict to this effect issued in the 26th year of his reign was engraved upon bronze plates. Later an edict issued by the

Second Emperor in the first year (209 BC) of his reign was added on the plates. Some of these plates were inlaid into bronze or iron measures; some had holes in the four corners or along the sides and were nailed upon wooden measures.

72. Tiger tally of Yangling Relic of Qin, 8.9 cm long, 2.1 cm wide, 3.4 cm high. This was a tally used by the First Emperor to move troops. It was made of bronze cast in the shape of a tiger and divided into two halves along the middle. An imperial edict of 12 characters in seal script was inlaid in gold on both the left and the

right side of the neck and back of the tiger. It reads in translation: "Tally for (moving) soldiers; the right half is in the emperor's hands, the left half at Yangling." It meant that the emperor kept the right half of the tally and gave the left half to the army commander at Yangling (east of modern Xianyang City, Shaanxi). When he wanted to move the troops there, he would send a messenger with his order and the right half of the tally to Yangling. The order would not be considered valid unless the two halves of the tally matched.

73-1

73. Silver dish of Xianyang Palace

Vessel for holding water, relic of Qin, diameter 37 cm, height 5.5 cm; unearthed from Pit 1 holding funerary objects in the tomb of the Prince of Qi of Western Han, in Lingzi District, Zibo, Shandong Province, in 1978—1980. The dish is ornamented with gilt dragon designs in the style of the Warring States Period. Originally it belonged to one of the six states that were conquered by the Qin. When the First Emperor obtained the dish, he added the date "thirty-third year" in Qin seal script under the rim and kept it in Xianyang Palace. After Liu Bang, first emperor of Han, occupied Xianyang he took the dish to his own palace. Later he bequeathed it to the Prince of Qi, who had been made a vassal at Zibo, which was why it was found in the prince's tomb.

73-2

74. Perspective drawing of Xianyang Palace The site of Xianyang Palace of Qin was excavated in 1975. It is located on the eastern outskirts of modern Xianyang City, Shaanxi Province. Xianyang was the capital of Qin from 354—206 BC. It was razed when the Qin Dynasty was overthrown. Unearthed at the palace site is a multilayered platform of rammed earth. What remains of it is 6 meters high, 60 meters from east to west, and 45 meters from north to south. The original halls and chambers were built on and around this platform.

75. Hollow brick with dragon designs Building material of Qin, 100 cm long, 38 cm wide, 16.5 cm thick; unearthed at Site 1 of the Qin palace grounds on the eastern outskirts of Xianyang City, Shaanxi Province, in 1974—75. Hollow bricks first appeared during the Warring States Period and were used mainly in the construction of palaces, government buildings and tombs. Its use reached a climax during the Western Han. There is an ancient Chinese theory that may be translated as "the cycle of five virtues," which are symbolized by metal, wood, water, fire and earth. The theory held that the Xia Dynasty was represented by the virtue of wood, the Shang Dynasty by the virtue of metal, and the Zhou Dynasty by the virtue of fire. When Shang replaced Xia, it was a case of metal winning against wood, and when Zhou replaced Shang, it was fire overcoming metal. The First Emperor of Qin, basing his thinking on a legend that a duke of Qin, called Wen, had captured a black dragon during a hunting trip, theorized that Qin had been blessed with the virtue of water, so when Qin replaced Zhou it was water extinguishing fire. The dragon designs on hollow bricks appear to be a reflection of this theory.

75

Map of Highways Built in the Qin Dynasty

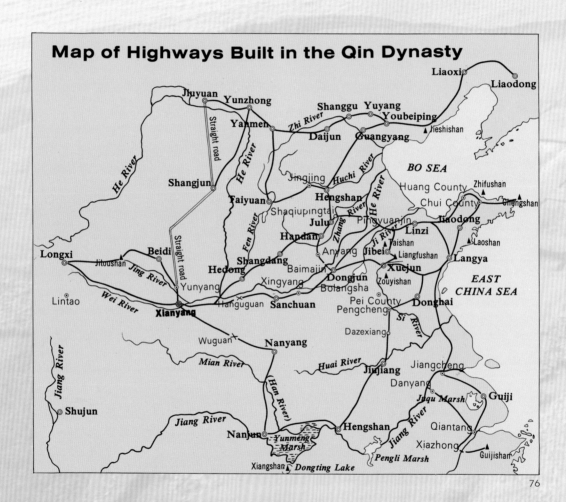

Liaoxi
Liaodong
Jiuyuan   Yunzhong
Shanggu Yuyang
Yanmen   Youbeiping
Zhi River   Jieshishan
Daijun   Guangyang
He River   Huchi River   BO SEA
Shangjun   Yingjing   Huang County   Zhifushan
He River   Chui County   Chengshan
Taiyuan   Hengshan
Shaqiupingtai   He River
Fen River   Julu   Pingyuanjin   Liaodong
Handan   Zhang River Ji River Linzi
Longxi   Beidi   Anyang   Jibei Taishan   Laoshan
Jitoushan Jing River Shangdang   Liangfushan   Langya
Straight road Hedong   Xuejun
Wei River Yunyang Xingyang Baimajin Dongjun Zouyishan EAST
Lintao   Hanguguan Sanchuan Bolangsha   CHINA SEA
Xianyang   Pei County Donghai
Pengcheng   Si River
Wuguan   Nanyang   Dazexiang
Mian River   Huai River   Jiujiang Jiangcheng
Jiang River   Danyang
(Han River)   Juqu Marsh   Guiji
Shujun   Jiang River   Qiantang
Nanjun   Yunmeng   Hengshan   Xiazhong
Xiangshan Marsh Dongting Lake Pengli Marsh   Guijishan

76. Map of highways built in the Qin Dynasty   After he conquered the six other states of the Warring States Period, the First Emperor ordered the removal of all passes and forts that obstructed free transportation. With his capital, Xianyang, as the starting point he had two major highways built, one running east through present-day Hebei and Shandong provinces to the shores of the Bo Sea, the other south to the present provinces of Jiangsu and Zhejiang. They were wide, well-built roads lined with pines. He also ordered his general Meng Tian to build what was called a straight road from Xianyang northward through Yunyang and Shangdu to Jiuyuan (north of modern Baotou City in the Inner Mongolia Autonomous Region). These highways and the straight road helped to consolidate the unified multiethnic country and facilitated economic and cultural interflow.

77-1

77. Inscribed stone of Langya Mountain

Relic of Qin; what still remains of it is 132.2 cm high, 65.8-71.3 cm wide and 36.2 cm thick. In 219 BC the First Emperor, during a second inspection trip through the country, climbed up Langya Mountain (south of Jiaonan, Shandong). He ordered the construction of the Langya Terrace and had his merits in unifying China inscribed on a piece of stone. The inscription is in Qin seal style and is said to be in the handwriting of Li Si, a court official accompanying the emperor on the trip. The complete text of the inscription has been included in Sima Qian's *Records of the Historian: Annals of the First*

Emperor of Qin. However, only 87 characters in 13 lines still remain on the stone and they are now illegible. The first two lines give the names and ranks of officials who accompanied the emperor on the trip; the other 11 lines contain an edict issued by the Second Emperor in 209 BC and the names of officials accompanying him. The stone originally stood on a cliff in the mountain. During the Qing Dynasty it was dug up and taken away by someone who preserved it as a valuable piece of relic with data important to an understanding of Qin's unification of China.

77-2

Examples of Different Ways of Writing
Chinese Characters During the Warring States Period

	peace	horse	positive	level	city
Qi character					
Chu character					
Yan character					
Han character					
Zhao character					
Wei character					
Qin character					
Eng. trans.	peace	horse	positive	level	city

78

78. Qin's unification of the Chinese written language   People wrote and spoke very differently in different parts of China during the Warring States Period, a situation that has been summed up in the saying, "The spoken word differed in sound, the written word differed in form." After unifying the country, the First Emperor abolished the classic scripts of the various feudal states and the variant forms of writing in different localities. Using the Qin script as the base and making reference to the scripts of the six other states, he created what was called the "small seal script," in which the characters were fixed in form, had few and simple strokes and were easy to write, and made it the standard script for the whole country. Shortly afterwards Cheng Miao, a county official, on the basis of forms of writing in general use by the people, invented square characters that were even simpler and easier to write. This style of writing, called *lishu*, or official script, established the basic structure of modern square Chinese characters. The unification of language during the Qin was a major contribution to the longterm stability of China's written language. It also helped to promote economic and cultural interflow and development in the country.

79. Remnants of stone inscriptions on Taishan   These are rubbings made in the Ming Dynasty. In 219 BC the First Emperor, during his second inspection trip through the country, ascended Taishan (Mount Tai in Tai'an City, Shandong), performed an ancient ritual called *feng-chan there,* and ordered that his merits be inscribed on a stone in the mountain. The full text of his inscriptions is included in the *Records of the Historian: Annals of the First Emperor of Qin.* The original inscriptions were carved on the four sides of a stone. The ones on three sides were done in the First Emperor's time; on the fourth side was an edict issued by the Second Emperor in 209 BC when he visited Jun County and the names of officials accompanying him. The inscriptions are in the same style as those

80

on the Langya stone — the small seal style adopted after Qin's unification of the Chinese language — and are said to be in the hand of the same man, Li Si. They are important documentary materials of the Qin Dynasty, but the characters are no longer clear. Only 29 characters were legible by the Ming Dynasty and only 10 by the Qing. As to rubbings, the best preserved is the complete rubbing made in the Northern Song, of which 165 characters still remain. It is now preserved in the Dai Temple of Tai'an, Shandong.

80. Brick with 12 characters in small seal script Floor tile of Qin, length 30.8 cm, width 26.7 cm, thickness 4 cm. The obverse side of the brick is divided into 12 squares by raised lines; each square bears a character inscribed in relief in Qin seal style, from which it may be assumed that the brick is a relic of the Qin Dynasty. The 12 characters say: "Loyal subjects everywhere; bumper harvests every year; no hungry men on the streets," a eulogy of the achievements of the Qin Dynasty.

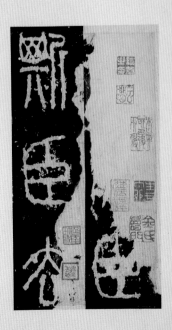

Sketch Map of the Ling Canal Dug in the Qin Dynasty

Simengan

Chetian Ling Canal

Li River

Rongjiangzhen

South Xing'an Canal

North Canal

Huazui

Xiang River

Jiangling Wuhan

Jiang River

Linxiang

Ling Canal

Xiang River

Li River

Fanyu

ᴧᴧᴧ Ling Canal

○ Present place-name

○ Seat of prefectural government

81

81. Sketch map of the Ling Canal dug in the Qin Dynasty Ling Canal, now called Xing'an Canal, is located in Xing'an County, Guangxi Zhuang Autonomous Region. When the First Emperor of Qin unified Lingnan (an area covering present-day Guangdong and Guangxi), he ordered Shilu to dig the canal for transportation of grain. The canal, with a total length of 34 kilometers, was completed in 214 BC. It is one of the oldest man-made canals in the world. It diverts the waters of the Xiang River in the north to the Li River in its south, joining two major river systems, the Yangtze and the Pearl. It was a key navigation canal linking the Central Plains and Lingnan in the old days, and a strategic project that ensured the First Emperor's control over Lingnan.

82. Half-tael coins and casting mold of the Qin Dynasty After his conquest of the six states, the First Emperor of Qin unified the country's currency by issuing two kinds of coins for exclusive circulation nationwide:the gold coin *shangbi* and the copper half-tael *xiabi* that is round with a square hole in the middle. He banned all currencies of the former six states. The half-tael coin is 3-3.6cm in diameter and weighs about 8 grams. On the obverse side are the two characters for "half tael" in relief. Historical records say that "the weight of the coin is as stated," meaning that it weighed half a tael under the Qin weight system. This round coin with a square hole was used up to the beginning of the 20th century. The mold was for making the coin.

82

83. Bronze *liang* Measures of Qin; the oval one is 30.2 cm long and the rectangular one 24.3 cm. To facilitate the computing of government taxes on grain, silk and other goods and unify calculations in civil engineering projects, in 221 BC the First Emperor of Qin decided to unify the country's weights and measures. Inscribed on the outside walls of the two bronze measures shown here is a 40-character imperial edict on the unification of weights and measures issued by the First Emperor in the 26th year of his reign. They are standard weight measures of the Qin Dynasty.

83-1

83-2

84. Pottery *liang* Measure of Qin, height 9.4 cm, diameter 20.4 cm, capacity 2,000 ml; unearthed in Zou County, Shandong Province, in 1963. Measures of the Qin Dynasty were made of bronze, pottery or wood. The outside wall of this pottery measure bears a 40-character imperial edict on the unification of weights and measures issued in the 26th year of the reign of the First Emperor of Qin. Large numbers of such pottery measures have been unearthed. They were standard measures in those days.

84

85-1

85-2

85. Eight-catty bronze *quan* Weight of Qin, height 5.5 cm, base diameter 9.8 cm, weight 2,063.5 grams. *Quan* was a weight used on a balance. Qin weights were made of bronze or iron. Inscribed on the body of the weight shown here is a 40-character imperial edict on the unification of weights and measures issued in the 26th year of the reign of the First Emperor. There is also an inscription of two characters in relief that reads in translation, "Eight catties." Tests show that a catty in those days is equivalent to 257.925 modern grams.

86-1

86-2

86. Big iron *quan* Weight of Qin, height 19 cm, base diameter 26 cm, weight 32.5 kgs; unearthed in Zuoyun County, Shanxi Province, in 1956. Set into one side of the body is a 40-character imperial edict on the unification of weights and measures issued in the 26th year of the reign of the First Emperor. Judging from its shape and the style of the inscription on it, this weight was probably cast in the 26th year of the reign of the First Emperor. It is the heaviest among all weights of Qin known or discovered so far.

87. Map of the Great Wall of the Qin Dynasty To guard against invasion and harassment by neighboring states and the nomadic tribes in the north, the larger feudal states of the Warring States Period built walls along their borders and on their northern frontiers. In 215 BC the First Emperor of Qin ordered General Meng Tian to lead an army of 300,000 to fight the Xiongnu in the north. After recovering the areas south of the Great Bend of the Yellow River, he carried out an extensive project of reconstruction and

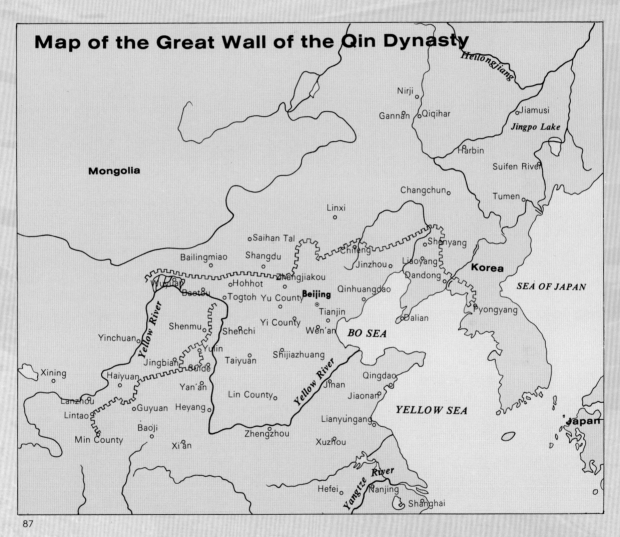

Map of the Great Wall of the Qin Dynasty

87

repair of the northern walls built by the former states of Qin, Zhao and Yan, linking them together to form one great wall that extended thousands of kilometers from Lintao (now Min County, Gansu Province) in the west to Liaodong in the east, a formidable defense line against Xiongnu invasion. Thanks to continued reconstruction and repairs in later generations, the imposing 10,000 *li* (5,000 kilometers) Great Wall has become one of the greatest architectural wonders in world history.

Harsh Rule with Severe Punishments

The Qin emperors ruled tyrannically, exacted heavy unpaid labor, and instituted severe forms of punishment. In 209 BC Chen Sheng and Wu Guang, two peasants forced by the Second Emperor to go north to garrison the country's frontiers, incited the masses to rebel on the way. "Felling trees to make weapons and raising the banner of revolt," they launched the first large-cale peasant uprising in Chinese history. Revolt against Qin tyranny soon engulfed the whole country and just three years later, in 206 BC, the Qin Dynasty was overthrown.

88. Square and circular bronze structural members   Relics of Qin, unearthed from the ruins of Epang Palace at Xiaosu Village, Chang'an County, Shaanxi Province, in 1974. The square member is 19 cm long, 14 cm wide and 7 cm high. In the middle is a shallow round pit with a diameter of 9.4 cm and a depth of 3.6 cm, into which the end of a door post was probably inserted. The circular member is hollow, height 9.3 cm, diameter 11.4 cm. To judge from its configuration, it may have been a member for joining and fastening wooden architectural parts. Both members were used in the construction of Epang Palace.

89. Restoration of Epang Palace   After conquering the six states, the First Emperor of Qin conscripted several hundred thousand workers to build his own palaces. Epang Palace, the front hall of the palace complex, was the first to be built. *Records of the Historian: Annals of the First Emperor of Qin* says that Epang Palace was a two-story building, measuring 500 *bu* (about 1,000

88

meters)from east to west and 50 *zhang* (about 165 meters) from north to south. The upper floor could seat 10,000 people and the lower floor was high enough to accommodate a 60-foot flagpole. On all sides were plank roads linked to each other. There were partition walls in the east, west and north. It was a magnificent and gigantic project that was still unfinished by the end of the Qin Dynasty. The parts that had been built were burned down in battles and now lie in ruins at present-day Sanqiaozhen, western suburbs of Xi'an, Shaanxi Province, on a high rectangular platform of rammed earth, measuring about 1,300 meters from east to west and 400 meters from south to north, and covering an area of 5.2 hectares. They provide important material for the study of Qin architecture.

90. Tile-ends with sunflower designs Building materials of Qin, diameter 13.5cm and 14.4 cm respectively; unearthed from the ruins of Epang Palace, Chang'an County, Shaanxi Province, in 1975. Tile-ends with sunflower designs were found among the tile-ends of the Qin Dynasty, but were much fewer than those with cloud designs. Like the tile-ends with designs of animals, leaves and whorls, and those with characters that connote auspiciousness, they are expressions of praise for the Qin Dynasty and the First Emperor for his unification of the country. Though the magnificent buildings of Xianyang Palace, Epang Palace and the Mausoleum of the First Emperor have disappeared, the large quantities of tile-ends that remain reflect the prosperity of the Qin Dynasty and the scale of its architecture.

89

90-1

90-2

91

91. Big tile-end Building material of Qin, diameter about 40 cm; discovered in the area of the Mausoleum of the First Emperor of Qin, Lintong, Shaanxi Province, in 1956. The tile-end bears a *kui*-phoenix design, vigorous looking and large in size. Another tile-end unearthed in the same area in 1977 is 48 cm high, with a diameter of 61 cm; it was the remnant of a cylindrical tile 32 cm long, the biggest tile yet known. These unusually large tile-ends give us some idea of the grandeur and magnificence of the Mausoleum of the First Emperor.

92. Tile-ends with cloud designs
Building materials of Qin, diameter 15.5 cm and 16.5 cm respectively; unearthed within the area of the Mausoleum of the First Emperor of Qin, Lintong, Shaanxi Province, in 1974. Tile-ends first appeared in the Western Zhou Dynasty and were widely used in the Qin and Han. The tile-end is the lowest part of a cylindrical tile; its use is to prevent eaves from being soaked by water. It also serves as a decoration. Tile-ends with cloud designs made up the majority of tile-ends unearthed from the ruins of Qin palaces. They were evidently the most popular at the time.

92-1

92-2

93. Iron pincers and fetters Instruments of torture, Qin Dynasty; unearthed from the ruins of a stone processing workshop of the Qin Dynasty, Zhengzhuang, Lintong, Shaanxi Province, in 1973. The iron pincers is 18 cm long, 2 cm wide and 0.8 cm thick, and was placed around the neck of a prisoner. The fetters are 38 cm long. Each hoop is 3 cm wide, 1 cm thick, and 8 cm in diameter. On one of the hoops is a lock. They were used to shackle a prisoner's feet. The east end of the stone processing workshop where these instruments were unearthed was linked to the northern end of the outside wall of the Mausoleum of the First Emperor of Qin, suggesting that the workshop was a temporary shelter for making building stones for the mausoleum. In the 35th year (212 BC) of the reign of the First Emperor, over 700,000 prisoners were despatched to the site to build Epang Palace and the Mausoleum. The iron pincers and fetters shown here were worn by the prisoners who made the building stones.

94. Inscriptions on tiles buried in tombs Relics of Qin, unearthed in Lintong, Shaanxi Province. In 1980, 32 graves of Qin Dynasty prisoners were excavated by a group of archaeologists at Zhaobeihu Village, west of the Mausoleum of the First Emperor of Qin. From these graves 100 skeletons were unearthed. Most of them were of young and middle-aged men, some of whom were slaughtered and then buried. Some of the skeletons were covered with broken pieces of flat or cylindrical tiles, parts of which were inscribed with characters. They recorded a prisoner's name, native place, rank and

the form of punishment. One of the two tiles shown here is 4.9 cm high and 3.9 cm wide. It bears an inscription of nine characters which tell us the prisoner's name was Ya, a native of Bianli Village at Lanling (now Lanlingzhen,Cangshan County, Shandong Province). He was a peer of the fourth rank (called a *bugeng* in the Qin Dynasty), and was sentenced to forced labor because he had committed a crime or owed money to the government. The other tile bears the inscriptions Dajiao (name of prisoner), Yangmin (his native place in the vicinity of today's Ningjin County, Hebei), and *juzi*, an expression meaning the prisoner had committed a crime or owed money to the government. These inscriptions show that the laborers taking part in the construction of the Mausoleum of the First Emperor were conscripted from different parts of the country.

93

94

The Western and Eastern Han Dynasties

(202 BC-AD 220)

In 202 BC Liu Bang, who joined the peasant uprising in the late Qin and won final victory in the wars between the Chu and Han, established the Han Dynasty and made Chang'an (today's Xi'an, Shaanxi Province) his capital. Historians called it the Western Han. In its early years, the Western Han government adopted a policy of recuperating and building up the strength of the nation. It quelled local separatist revolts and expedited the recovery and development of the social economy. By the time of Emperor Wu the unified, multiethnic feudal country had been further consolidated and the Han Dynasty was at its zenith. In the late Western Han, however, struggles among local despots for annexation of land intensified and social contradictions became increasingly acute. In AD 8 Wang Mang, a relative on the maternal side of the imperial family, proclaimed himself emperor and established the Xin Dynasty to replace the Han. He tried to carry out reforms to lift the country out of a critical situation but failed, and in AD 23 his dynasty was overthrown by peasant uprisings known as the Green Woodsmen and Red Eyebrows.

In AD 25 Liu Xiu, a member of the Han royal house who had taken part in peasant uprisings in the late Western Han, re-established the Han Dynasty with its capital at Luoyang (today's Luoyang, Henan Province); it was known in history as the Eastern Han. Powerful landlord forces formed in the late Western Han continued to expand under the new regime. They manipulated state power at all levels, owned and administered feudal manors, organized private armies, and ruthlessly exploited and oppressed the peasants. In AD 184 a peasant uprising on an unprecedented scale, the Uprising of Yellow Turbans, broke out. In AD 220 the Eastern Han was overthrown, and Cao Pi established the Wei Dynasty, proclaiming himself emperor.

The Powerful and Prosperous Western Han

In the early years of the Western Han, the policies of governing by noninterference (in local administrative work) and of recuperating and building up the strength of the country conduced to a rapid recovery of the social economy. During the reign of Emperor Wu, centralized state power was tightened and the unified multiethnic country was able to develop and consolidate.

Rehabitation in the Early Years of the Western Han

Learning from the rapid downfall of the Qin regime, the early rulers of Western Han carried out a policy of letting the people relax and recuperate; as a result the sagging social economy was able to revive and develop. And with the crackdown on local separatist forces the unity of the country was further strengthened.

95. Lesser half-tael copper coins Currency of Western Han, diameter 2.3 cm;unearthed at Houchuan, Shaan County, Henan Province, in 1956. In the early years of the Western Han Dynasty the Han government retained the currency system of the previous Qin Dynasty and continued to mint half-tael-copper coins. At the same time it allowed vassal lords and industrial and commercial magnates to mint coins on their own, thus accelerating the recovery and development of the economy. As the half-tael coin of the Western Han was lighter than that of the Qin Dynasty, it was commonly called the lesser half-tael. It was the principal form of money of the early Western Han.

96

96. Tile-end inscribed with characters that read, in translation, "Han unified the country"
Building material of Western Han, diameter 17.5 cm; unearthed at the site of the Han city of Chang'an, Xi'an, Shaanxi Province. After the Qin Dynasty was overthrown, Xiang Yu of Chu and Liu Bang of Han fought for control over the country. After four years of war, during which dozens of battles, great and small, were fought, Liu Bang allying himself with all forces opposing Xiang Yu succeeded in entrapping the latter's army at Gaixia (present-day Haocheng, Guzhen County, Anhui). Defeated and with no hope for aid, the Chu chief committed suicide. Liu Bang, the victor, then established the Han Dynasty. This tile-end with the inscription Han unified the country-was made to commemorate Liu Bang's victory over Xiang Yu, the reunification of the country, and the founding of the Han Dynasty. Such tile-ends have also been unearthed at the ruins of Jianzhang Palace built during the reign of Emperor Wu of Han.

97. Stone pig and piglets　Burial objects of Western Han, unearthed outside the Southern Gate of Changsha, Hunan Province, in 1956. The large pig is 18.3 cm long and the small ones are 4.9 cm , 4.5 cm and 3.7 cm respectively. Raising pigs, chiefly in pens, was popular in the Han Dynasty. Local officials encouraged people to engage in farming and sericulture, often calling on each household to raise two female pigs and five chickens, or one pig and four hens. Placing a stone pig in each hand of the deceased was a funeral custom in those days.

98

98. Pottery model of granary　Burial object of Western Han, height 34.5 cm, mid-body diameter 20 cm; unearthed at Fenghuangshan, Jiangling County, Hubei Province, in 1975. To change the autocratic rule of the Qin Dynasty, the early rulers of Western Han adopted the policies of "governing by noninterference"and "giving people a respite", which accelerated the recovery and development of the nation's economy. Granaries were filled to overflow, often to an extent that the grain rotted. When excavated, this model of a granary contained four ears of grain in bright yellow color, evidence that rice was an important staple food in the region and that the economy had sufficiently recovered.

97

99. Clay figurines of warriors from the tomb of a king of Chu Burial objects of Western Han; unearthed in a burial pit adjacent to the tomb of a king of Chu at Shizishan, Xuzhou, Jiangsu Province, in 1984. In the early years of the Western Han Dynasty, a parallel system of prefectures and fiefdoms was practised, that is, in addition to the setting up of prefectures and counties, some lords, with or without the same surname as the royal family, were granted fiefdoms. Thousands of painted clay figurines of warriors and horses have been unearthed at Shizishan. Most of the figurines were of foot soldiers. There were also some cavalrymen, but no chariots, an indication that chariots had lost their importance in the army by this time . This discovery is of great value to the study of the army and military system of the Western Han Dynasty.

100. Bronze *ge* (dagger-axe) with a gold *yue* (an ancient wind instrument)
Weapon of Western Han, 22.5 cm long; unearthed at Linzi, Zibo, Shandong Province, between 1978 and 1980. In the early years of the Western Han Dynasty, the state of Qi was very powerful militarily. After the death of Liu Bang and his wife Empress Lü, members of the Lü family, the empress' kinsmen, seized power and attempted a rebellion against the Han. Liu Xiang, a scion of Liu Bang who was titled Prince Ai of Qi, stationed an army at Jinan to support the Han cause and, together with the forces of the Han court, put down the rebellion. Large numbers of weapons have been discovered among the funerary objects in his tomb. The bronze dagger-axe shown here is similar in shape to dagger-axes of the Warring States Period. It had a golden adjunct shaped like a tube wind instrument, at the top of which is the figure of a mandarin duck with its head turned back. A masterpiece in craftsmanship of the Western Han, weapons like this axe were probably used mainly by members of the palace guard.

101. Gilded bronze crossbow Weapon of Western Han, 15 cm long, 16.6 cm wide; unearthed at Linzi, Zibo, Shandong Province between 1978 and 1980. The bronze crossbow first appeared in the early Warring States Period and was gradually improved during the Han. It had a bronze case, in which were a sight similar to the rearsight in a modern sighting device, a trigger, a pawl and two axis holes linking the various parts to form a well-integrated mechanism. This crossbow was corroded by rust, parts of the gold has fallen off, and some parts of the mechanism are lost. Nevertheless, it suffices to show the basic structure and workmanship of crossbows of the Han Dynasty. On the bow are some characters referring to an official named He who was in charge of the making of the weapon.

102. Long iron *pi* and bronze *zun*
Weapons of Western Han, unearthed at Linzi, Zibo , Shandong Province between 1978 and 1980. The head of the *pi* (spearlike weapon with sharply pointed head and two cutting edges) is 72 cm long and the hoop is 13.3 cm. The *zun* (butt of spear) is 28 cm long. When first discovered, the shaft of the *pi* had rotted. Its full length, after restoration, is 2.9 meters. The *pi* was an advanced weapon of its time, deadlier than most other weapons. It could be used both as a spear and as a sword. The number of *pi* recovered from the tomb of a prince of Qi was second only to that of halberds, which shows their important place among weapons of the Western Han.

101

102

◁ 100

103. Map showing the suppression of the Seven-Prince Rebellion by Emperor Jing of Han Early in the wars between the states of Chu and Han, Liu Bang, in order to unite all forces opposing Xiang Yu of Chu, conferred on Han Xin, Peng Yue and five other warlords the title of prince. After the establishment of the Western Han Dynasty, to consolidate the rule of the Han royal court, he removed six of the princes whose surnames were different from the royal family's and gave their princedoms to members of the Liu family, hoping thus to strengthen his control over the provinces. It turned out, however, that the newly created princes rapidly expanded their power and soon

became a real threat to the central government. Then, in 154 BC, Prince Liu Bi of Wu, allying himself with the six princes of Chu, Zhao, Jiaodong, Jiaoxi, Jinan and Zichuan, rose in rebellion against the Han. Emperor Jing, the reigning Han emperor, ordered Marshal Zhou Yafu to lead an army against the rebels, who were suppressed in a little over two months. The victory further strenghtened centralized state power and safeguarded both the unity of the country and social stability. Thereafter, the power of the feudal princes was reduced; they were not allowed to have a hand in the country's political affairs.

104. Painted pottery figurines of foot soldiers and cavalrymen Burial objects of Western Han, unearthed from a burial pit in Chang Ling, a royal tomb at Yangjiawan, Xianyang, Shaanxi Province, in 1965. The foot soldiers are 48-50 cm tall and the mounted men 54-68 cm tall. Over 2,500 painted pottery figurines were unearthed from the pit, including some 1,800 infantrymen, 580 cavalrymen and models of war chariots. They were arranged in imitation of a battle formation that reflects the transition from the use of cavalry and chariots to the use of infantry as the main force in battle.

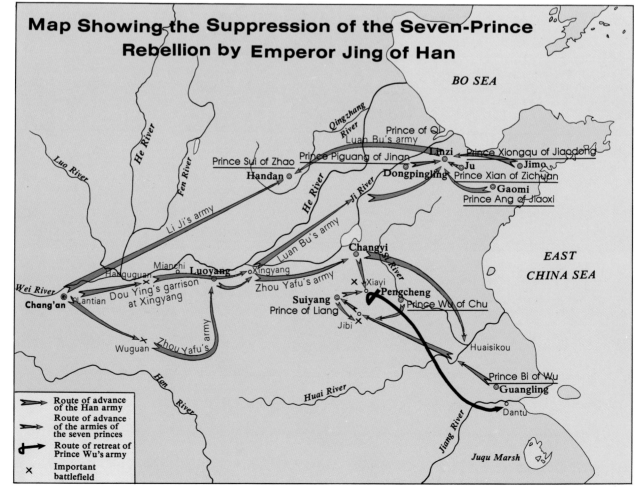

Consolidation and Development of Centralized State Power

After succeeding to the throne, Emperor Wu continued to reduce the power of local separatist regimes. He stationed envoys in the Western Regions, launched large-scale counterattacks against the Xiongnu, enforced state management of the salt and iron industry, decreed a state monopoly on the mintage of coins, undertook many water conservancy projects, promoted advanced agricultural techniques, and proscribed all non-Confucian schools of thought, espousing Confucianism as the orthodox state ideology. The Han Dynasty reached its zenith during his reign.

105. Portrait of Emperor Wu of the Han Dynasty   Liu Che, or Emperor Wu (156-87 BC), was an outstanding statesman of ancient China. At the age of four he was made the prince of Jiaodong, and at seven became crown prince. He succeeded to the throne at sixteen. During his long reign (141-87 BC) he suppressed local separatist forces, instituted a state monopoly on the production and sale of salt and iron and on the mintage of coins, undertook water conservancy projects, promoted agricultural production, and launched large-scale counterattacks against the Xiongnu (Huns) who had encroached upon the borders of his empire. He espoused Confucianism, tightened ideological control, strengthened ties among the different nationalities in the country, and promoted intercourse with countries and regions abroad. All these measures helped

105

to consolidate the system of centralized power and expedited the development of the unified, multiethnic feudal country. His reign ushered in a period of prosperity for the Western Han Dynasty.

106. Sketch map of Chang'an City in the Han Dynasty   Chang'an was the capital of the Western Han. It was approximately a square, but with some bends and turnings in its northern and southern walls. The total length of the walls was 25 kilometers. There were three city gates on each side and three passageways in each gate, through which 12 chariots could pass at the same time. Wide streets extended from eight of the gates, leading to the interior of the city. These were the city's main roads. They were 45 meters wide and about 3,000 meters long. The longest, Anmen Road, was 5,500 meters long. Inside the city were imperial palaces, government offices and arsenals, as well as commercial and handicraft districts and residential areas with local-style dwelling houses. The city had a population of 240,000 by the end of the Western Han, the most populous city in the world at the time.

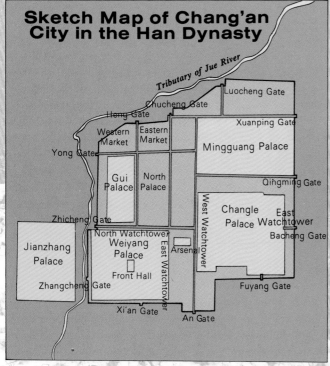

Sketch Map of Chang'an City in the Han Dynasty

106

107

107. Tile-end with the characters "Heaven's mandate for Chanyu"
Building material of Western Han, diameter 17.1 cm; unearthed from a Han tomb at Zhaowan, Baotou, Inner Mongolia Autonomous Region, in 1955. The Xiongnu (Huns) were a nomadic tribe on the Mongolian highlands who lived by hunting. They often intruded into the country's interior, looting money and goods and carrying off people as captives.

Though a constant menace to the life and property of the people and to the stability of the Han regime, the Han imperial court, in its early years, was unable to launch large-scale military expeditions against them. It was not until the reign of Emperor Wu when the country's economic situation had much improved and its military strength had greatly expanded that all-out counteroffensives could be made. Using such able generals as Wei

Qing and Huo Qubing, Emperor Wu fought more than ten fierce battles with the Xiongnu over a period of ten years, driving back the intruders and bringing security to both agricultural production and the life of the people in north China. "Chanyu" was a title used by a Xiongnu chieftain. The tile-end with the inscription "Heaven's mandate for Chanyu" was made to praise the success of the Han troops in repulsing the intrusions of Xiongnu chiefs.

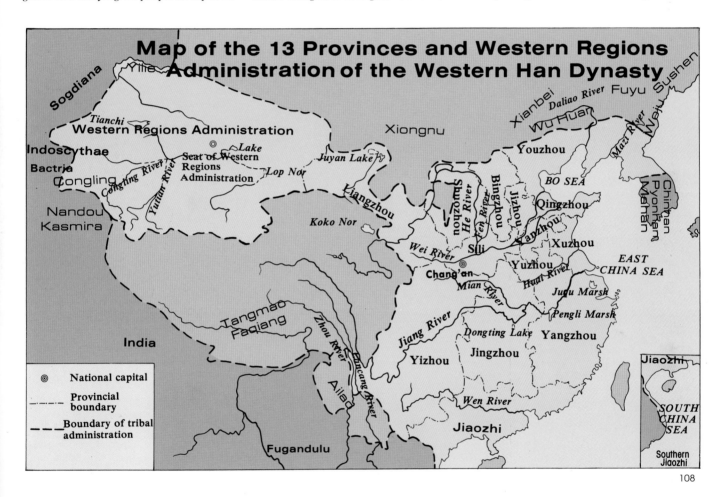

108

108. Map of the 13 provinces and Western Regions Administration of the Western Han Dynasty To strengthen his control over the provinces Emperor Wu of Han, in the fifth year of his reign titled Yuanfeng(106 BC), divided the whole country, including both prefectures and fiefdoms, into 13 provinces each governed by an official appointed by the central government. The duty of the governor

was to supervise local officials and keep an eye on despots. Half a century later Emperor Xuan, in the second year (60 BC) of his reign titled Shengjue, set up a Western Regions Administration at Wulei (Bugur, present-day Luntai County, Xinjiang Uygur Autonomous Region) and stationed high officials there to administer and protect the areas east and south of Lake Balkhash.

109. Iron spearhead and bronze knife with two edges Weapons of Western Han, unearthed from a Han tomb at Lingshan, Mancheng County, Hebei Province, in 1968. The spearhead is 21.9 cm long and the knife 15.8 cm long. The shaft of the spear has corroded, but by measuring the distance between the spearhead and the knife when they were unearthed, we may assume that the full length of the spear, including the shaft, was about 1.96 cm. During the reign of Emperor Wu of Western Han, iron spears improved quickly and bronze spears gradually went out of use. Iron spears were shorter and lighter than bronze ones, and their tips instead of being round were sharply pointed, making them much more deadly weapons in battle. This iron spearhead resembles a flat willow leaf. The narrow part of the bronze knife is inlaid with gold, an example of the fine workmanship of weapon makers in those days.

109-2

109-1

110

111

110. Iron halberd Weapon of Western Han, 33.7 cm long; unearthed at Houchuan, Shaan County, Henan Province, in 1956. The halberd, a weapon that could thrust, hook, stab and cut, was widely used in battle during the Han Dynasty. People in those days described military strength by the expression "armed with a million halberds," indicating that the number of soldiers using halberds was an important measure of the strength of an army. Halberds like the one shown here were the most common kind used by Han soldiers.

111. Tiger-shaped tally issued to Prefect of Zhangye A certificate with imperial authorization for troop movements, 5.6 cm long and 2.5 cm high; relic of Western Han. The use of bronze tiger-shaped tallies began in the ninth month of the second year (178 BC) of the reign of Emperor Wen of Western Han. A tally was divided into halves. The right half was kept in the capital and the left half in a prefecture. When the central government wanted to move an army into battle, it would dispatch an envoy carrying the right half of the tally to the prefecture. The prefect had to check if the right half matched the left half in his hands before the imperial order could become effective. Shown here is the left half of a tiger-shaped tally. On the left side of the tiger's body are four characters inlaid with silver that read in translation "Zhangye, left one." On its back is the left side of eight characters meaning "Tiger-shaped tally issued to the Prefect of Zhangye."

112

112. Mud seal with four characters meaning "Official Seal of Iron Industry of Qi"   Relic of Western Han, remnant 2.5 cm long. In ancient China when a person had written a document or letter on bamboo slips, he placed a piece of wood with a horizontal notch over the slips and tied them together with a string. Then he covered the knot in the string with mud and stamped it with a seal like the one shown here. This is the seal of an office set up by the state of Qi to manage the iron industry during the early years of the Western Han Dynasty.The four characters are in traditional seal script.

113. Pottery molds for casting ironware Relic of Western Han, unearthed in Teng County, Shandong Province. The salt and iron industries were the two principal production departments of the Western Han Dynasty. In 119 BC Emperor Wu of Han, acting on recommendations made by Sang Hongyang and others, placed the salt and iron industries operated by rich merchants under national control. He set up 36 state salt offices and 49 state iron offices to deal exclusively with the production and sale of these two commodities. These measures increased state revenue and reinforced centralized state power and the unity of the country. The pottery molds shown here carry the marks "Shanyang Two"and "Juye Two," indicating that they were molds used by the No.2 state-operated foundry at Shanyang Prefecture (later changed to Juye Prefecture during the reign of Wang Mang), present-day Juye County, Shandong Province.

114.Five-*zhu* copper coins of the reign of Emperor Wu of Han   Currency of Western Han, diameter about 2.3 cm, weight about 3.5 g. Emperor Wu of the Western Han enforced a state monopoly on mintage; all five-*zhu* coins were to be made by the central government. (*Zhu* was a unit of weight in ancient China. During the Han Dynasty, 24 *zhu* were equal to a tael and 16 taels to a catty.) Three officials under the *Shuiheng Duwei* (an inner court official in charge of imperial gardens, the wealth of the royal family and the mintage of coins) were appointed to take charge of the minting of five-*zhu* coins in the capital. One was in charge of minting; the other two were responsible for testing the color of the copper to be used and the carving of molds respectively. The coins were in high relief along the edges, had characters in the style of small seal script, and were used throughout the country. By and large, such coins were used for over 700 years from the Han Dynasty to the Sui Dynasty.

115.Copper mold for casting five-*zhu* coins   Relic of Western Han, 24.1 cm long, 9.5 cm wide; unearthed in Shouguang County, Shandong Province. In the early years of the Western Han Dynasty, coins minted by the state underwent many changes. Laws governing coin mintage were very confusing at the time, and privately-minted coins were also widely used. In 113 BC Emperor Wu, to meet the heavy outlay of years of war and to strengthen centralization in finance, adopted a policy of state monopoly on coin mintage. Five-*zhu* coins minted by the central government were made the

113-2

113-1

114

sole currency in the country; coin mintage by local authorities or individuals was forbidden; and various old coins were abolished. Monopoly of coin mintage by the central government restricted the expansion of local forces, increased state revenue, and consolidated the central government's rule. This copper mold was used to make five-*zhu* coins in a local mint prior to the enforcement of state monopoly on mintage.

115

Agriculture and Water Conservancy

Iron farm tools were widely used during the Western Han Dynasty. The government encouraged peasants to till land with oxen, and plowing techniques were greatly improved. Water conservancy projects were undertaken in many places at Guanzhong (the central Shaanxi plains), enlarging the acreage of farmland under irrigation and increasing agricultural production considerably. In the late years of the Western Han, land under cultivation reached 8 million Han *qing* and the country's population exceeded 50 million. (A Han *qing* is smaller than a modern *qing*, which is 6.66 ha.)

116. Big iron plowshare and plowshare with soil-digger   Farm implements of Western Han; unearthed in Liaoyang, Liaoning Province and Xianyang, Shaanxi Province respectively. Farming techniques made great progress in the Western Han Dynasty. The iron plowshare with cutting blade and soil-digger was a complex device that could break up and turn over the soil simultaneously. It was used to break up soil, dig furrows and raise ridges. As a big iron plowshare was very heavy, the rack of the plow had to be large too, thus increasing the weight of the plow. Generally, two or more strong oxen were needed to pull the plow, whether in digging ditches or turning up soil. This shows the great progress made in iron casting and agricultural production during the Han Dynasty.

116

117. Iron harrow Farm tool of Western Han, 16 cm long, 12 cm tall; unearthed from the ruins of a Han city in Chongan County, Fujian Province, in 1980. A hub of water transportation in these days, Chongan was an important community of the Yue nationality in Fujian Province. It was probably a "royal city" built by the Yue people during the Western Han. In addition to the harrow, other iron tools such as picks, spades and sickles were unearthed from the same ruins, evidence of material and cultural exchanges between the Han in the Central Plains and the Yue in Fujian Province. It also shows that during the Western Han Dynasty iron farm tools were widely used even in remote border areas.

117

118. Sketch of a drill barrow This drawing is based on the *Book of Agriculture* by Wang Zhen and on a mural painting in a Han tomb at Pinglu County, Shanxi Province. Reference was also made to an early type of three-legged barrow in the Nanyang area. Historical records say that the drill barrow was a new type of seed drill made by artisans under the guidance of Zhao Guo, an official in charge of agriculture during the reign of Emperor Wu of Han. When sowing, the peasant put seeds in a funnel linked to the hollow legs of a drill barrow; as he walked along, he would swing the funnel and the seeds would drop on the ground. Such a drill barrow could plow and sow at the same time and scatter seeds more evenly, thus providing for faster and better planting. Although drill barrows have only been seen in the murals of a Han tomb at Pinglu County, Shanxi Province, the iron legs of such barrows have been discovered at a number of places, such as Sandaohao of Liaoyang, Liaoning Province, Qinghe town of Beijing, and Fuping County of Shaanxi Province. It shows that drill sowing was fairly widespread in the Han Dynasty.

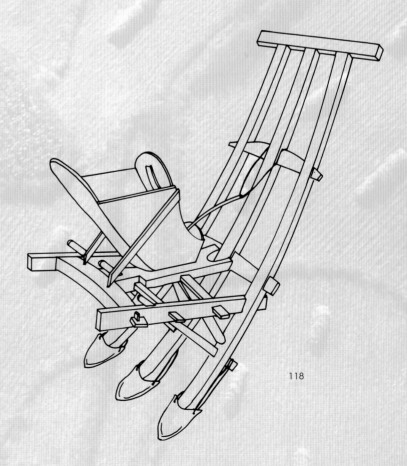

118

119. Pottery clay models of granaries for soya beans and barley with a capacity of half-million kilos each   Burial objects of Western Han, 43 cm and 44 cm high respectively; unearthed at Jinguyuan, Luoyang, Henan Province, in 1953. During the Western Han Dynasty, the kinds of crops grown by farmers increased gradually. *Ma* (an ancient grain, no longer cultivated), maize, millet, wheat, barley, beans and rice were the main food crops. Wheat and barley were widely planted, including both spring wheat and winter wheat, which were the most common cereals at the time. Varieties of beans such as soya beans, red beans and broad beans served not only as staple foods but also as non-staple foods and dressings. Written on the outside walls of the model granaries unearthed at Jinguyuan were characters in official style relating to maize, millet, soya beans, barley, etc.,a reflection of the unprecedented development of agriculture in the Western Han Dynasty.

120. Pottery model of a well with pulley and water trough Burial object of Western Han, 47.8 cm high; unearthed at Shaogou, Luoyang, Henan Province, in 1953. Wells for small-scale irrigation were common in the Western Han Dynasty. In the Central Plains people generally used a pulley to lift a large quantity of water from a deep well. This is a pottery model of a well with a water funnel, a water trough and a pulley. It is an example of well-irrigation in the Han Dynasty.

122-1

Handicraft Industry

The handicraft industry was highly developed in both production scale and technique during the Western Han. The main production categories included salt, iron, bronze, textile, lacquerware and pottery. Brightly colored silks and satins and exquisitely made lacquerware reached a high level technologically.

121. Deer-shaped bronze mat-weight inlaid with shell   Relic of Western Han, 9.8cm high; unearthed at Houchuan, Shaan County, Henan Province, in 1957. There was not much variation in Han Dynasty furniture. Even in a well furnished room there were usually nothing more than a low bed, a small table and a screen. But it was a custom to cover many parts of a room with mats. In order that the corners of a mat might not be creased when a person on the mat stood up or sat down abruptly, the corners were usually weighed down with heavy objects. Most such weights were made in the shape of animals. The deer was a popular image, for the Chinese character for deer *lu* has the same pronunciation as the character for official rank (also lu). The back of this deer-shaped bronze weight is inlaid with shell, a clever integration of usage with decoration.

122. Grain design jasper *bi*   Sacrificial or burial object of Western Han, diameter 26.3 cm. During the Pre-Qin era, the *bi* (jade disc with hole in the middle), *cong* (jade square with hole in the middle), *zhang* (jade with pointed tip) and *huang* (semicircular jade tablet) were called sacrificial and ritual jades, and were used at sacrificial ceremonies and during pilgrimages. Using jade for such purposes declined during the Han Dynasty, but the *bi* was still used on important occasions such as the *liao* (burning of wood as sacrifice to heaven) and chen (sinking jade as an offering to river gods). Sometimes the *bi* was also used as a burial object, being placed on the bosom or back of the deceased or between the inner and outer coffins, or inlaid into the outside wall of a coffin as a decoration. This *bi* has a design made of round granules as small as millet seeds, arranged in an orderly way and encircled with a *kui* dragon pattern. It is hard, sparkling and attractive, representative of the high level of jadecraft in the Han Dynasty.

121

122-2 ▷

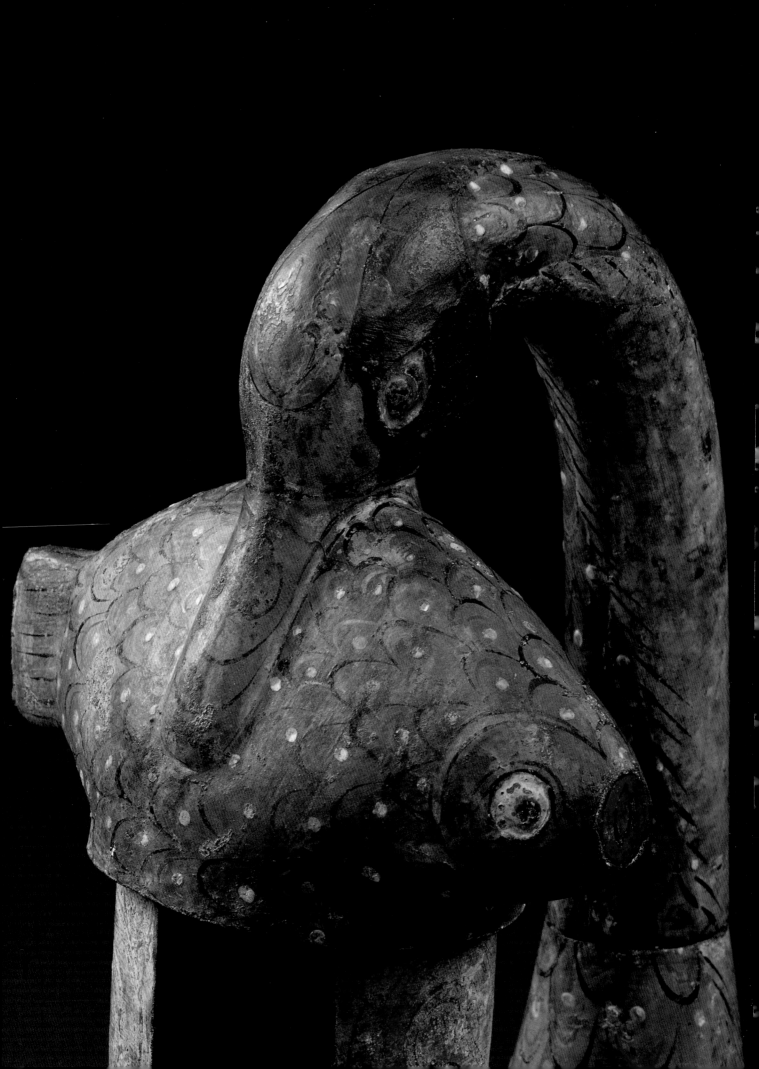

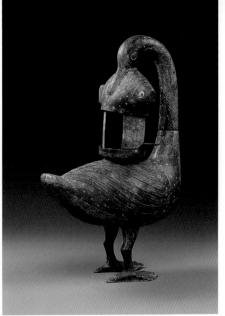

123-2

and the neck and body of the wild goose are hollow and connected to each other; they hold the smoke and ashes. All parts of the lamp are detachable, making it easy to clean them. The design is rational and ingeniously conceived, a perfect integration of the artistic and the practical.

123. Painted bronze lamp in the shape of a wild goose with fish in mouth Lighting device of Western Han, 53 cm tall; unearthed at Zhao Shibazhuang, Shuo County, Shanxi Province, in 1985. Bronze lamps of the Han Dynasty were varied in shape, exquisitely made and easy to use. Their forms usually connoted auspicious themes. There are, for example, lamps shaped like the leg of a wild goose, a scarlet bird, an ox or a ram. This wild-goose lamp used the traditional design of a bird with a fish in its mouth. The lamp plate and chimney can be moved to adjust the light and keep away the wind. The fish

124. Gilded bronze mat-weights shaped like bears Relics of Western Han, 5.2 cm tall; unearthed in Hefei, Anhui Province, in 1952. During the Han Dynasty, such weights were usually made of metal and small in size. To avoid getting entagled in clothes and other objects, a weight was usually shaped like a half-spheroid. An animal image, to be of such a shape, often had to be depicted in a squatting position. The two weights shown here are shaped like bears, a popular image during the Han Dynasty. A chubby bear, lovely, good-natured, but not clumsy, added life to the monotonously decorated homes of the Han Dynasty.

124

125-1

125. Jade clothes sewn with gold thread

Grave clothes of Western Han, 182 cm long; unearthed from Han Tomb No.40 at Bajiaolang Village, Ding County, Hebei Province, in 1973. People in the Han Dynasty believed that jade could preserve a corpse from decay. Therefore, some aristocrats after death were clad in jade clothes resembling armor. The clothes were made of jade pieces of different shapes and sizes, sewn together with metal thread. There are no specific records of

rules and regulations governing the use of jade clothes in the Western Han Dynasty, nor of the kinds and quality of the jade and thread. We know only from what has been discovered that gold, silver, copper and even silk threads were used. Rules on the use of jade clothes in the Eastern Han, however, were clearly defined in historical records: jade clothes sewn with gold thread were for emperors; silver threads were for vassal lords, marquis, court ladies and princesses; and copper threads for the emperor's sisters. In AD 222, the third year of the reign

titled Huangchu of the kingdom of Wei (one of the Three Kingdoms),a law was passed forbidding the use of jade clothes. The clothes shown here consisted of a total of 1,203 pieces of jade, sewn with 2,567 grams of gold thread. The occupant of the grave was Liu Xiu, Prince Huai of Zhongshan, who died in 55 BC. His tomb had been set on fire by grave robbers, but the jade clothes, though exposed to flames, appear to be brighter than usual.

125-2

127-1

126. Gilded bronze mirror bearing the inscription "Great Stability in China"

Relic of Xin, Wang Mang's regime, diameter 18.6 cm, edge thickness 0.6 cm; unearthed in Changsha, Hunan Province, in 1951. Bronze mirrors were widely used in the Han Dynasty. There was a rich variety of such mirrors, nearly all of exquisite workmanship. This mirror is gilded on the back and is decorated with figures of immortals and animals as well as regular patterns. The composition is a sophisticated one, the style is smooth and lively. It is a rare treasure among bronze mirrors with regular patterns of the Han Dynasty. Along the rim is an inscription of 53 characters that includes the slogan "Great Stability in China", an expression of the people's wish for a stable, prosperous and unified country.

127. Gilded bronze *zun* with bird-and-animal design
Wine vessel of Western Han, 14.6 cm high. New progress was made in the technique of casting bronzeware in the Han Dynasty. This is a cylindrical bronze *zun* with bear-shaped legs. On the lid are a ring and three flying birds, and on the bottom is an inscription inlaid with silver. It was gilded all over, and though much of the gilt has been rubbed away, it is nevertheless an example of the advanced art of gilding bronzeware in the Han Dynasty.

127-2

126-2

128. Bronze rhino-shaped *zun* inlaid with gold and silver cloud designs
Wine vessel of Western Han, 34.1 cm tall, 58.1 cm long; unearthed in Xingping County, Shaanxi Province, in 1963. In ancient China, quite a few bronze wine vessels were cast in the shape of animals, such as the ox *zun*, elephant *zun* and pig *zun* in Shang bronzeware, and pony *zun*, rabbit *zun* and duck *zun* in Zhou bronzeware. Beast-shaped *zun*, though not very much in vogue, was still popular in the Han Dynasty. This *zun* is an image of a rhinoceros with its head raised, a tough, muscular and vigorous creature with a well-proportioned body. It was modeled on the Suman rhinoceros that lived in ancient China. The whole vessel is inlaid with gold and silver cloud designs. Though made for general use, it is a work of art brimming with vitality, a wonder of the bronzeware of Western Han.

129-1

129-2

129. Bronze jar with inscriptions in bird script Wine or grain container of Western Han, height 40.5 cm; unearthed from Liu Sheng's tomb in Mancheng County, Hebei Province, in 1968. Bronze objects were cast on a large scale during the Han Dynasty. They were not only numerically great but of many varieties. Instead of the crude, clumsy and primitive features of Shang-Zhou bronzeware with their aura of mystery, Han objects were generally light and handy, catering to the needs of everyday life. Their designs were simple and plain, yet showed improvements in the techniques of gold and silver plating and of inlaying with gold, silver, glass and precious stones. On the body of the bronze jar shown here are 31 characters with auspicious meanings in bird script, ornamented with gold and silver filigree. The broad bands on the shoulder and belly of the jar are inlaid with vivid images of dragons and tigers fighting. All are exquisite works of art, examples of fine workmanship in metal in China 2,000 years ago.

130

131. Pottery rice-steamer on an iron caldron Cooking vessel of Western Han, height 20 cm, diameter of steamer's mouth 17 cm, diameter of bottom of caldron 5.5 cm; unearthed at Houchuan, Shaan County, Henan Province, in 1956. The techniques of iron smelting, casting and forging were greatly improved during the Western Han. There was a great variety of furnaces for blasting, smelting, forging, annealing, and for making wrought steel. They were made of fire-proof material, and were equipped with air-blowers and devices for reducing iron ores. The technique of using pig iron to make decarbonized steel had further developed, with noticeable increases in output. The discovery of this pottery rice-steamer sitting on an iron caldron shows that with the increase in metallurgical production, steel and iron were being used not only to make farm tools, hand tools and weapons, but also increasingly to make articles for daily use.

130. Lacquer ear-shaped cup of the empress' family in Changsha Wine vessel of Western Han, 11.4 cm long, 2.7 cm high; unearthed in Changsha, Hunan Province. The making of lacquerware reached a peak during the Western Han. Lacquer was used to coat everyday articles, furniture, musical instruments, utensils, burial objects, even parts of weapons and armor, for lacquered objects were not only light and beautiful but also durable. In general, wood or bamboo reinforced with ramie was used to make the roughcast, which was then surfaced with red or black lacquer. Designs, embossed or painted with lacquer or oils, were added on the surface. Sometimes a vessel was decorated with gold and silver foil or needle-incised patterns. Sometimes, to increase the durability, bronze, gold or silver inlay was added as complementary decoration. Aristocrats and high officials had a preference for using lacquerware in their homes. They used to mark a

conferred title or their surnames on the lacquerware. The background of the cup shown here is a light reddish brown, bearing a black lacquer painting of cloud-and-bird designs. Close to the bottom of the vessel are six characters that read, in translation, "Cup of the empress'family in Changsha", an indication of precious lacquerware owned by the nobility.

131

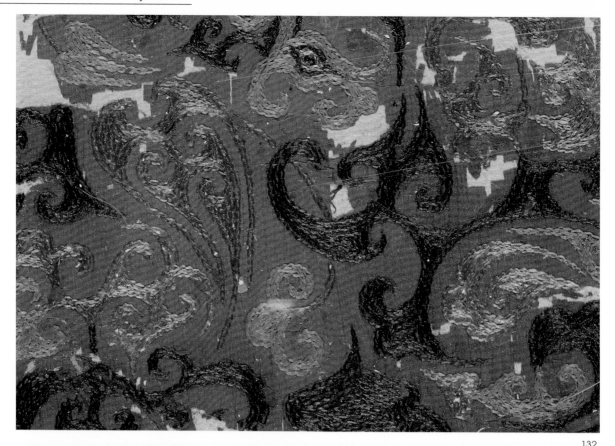

132

133

132. Embroidery with longevity pattern on deep-red thin, tough silk

133. Cornel embroidery on thin, tough silk

134. "Riding the clouds" embroidery on yellowish brown thin, tough silk

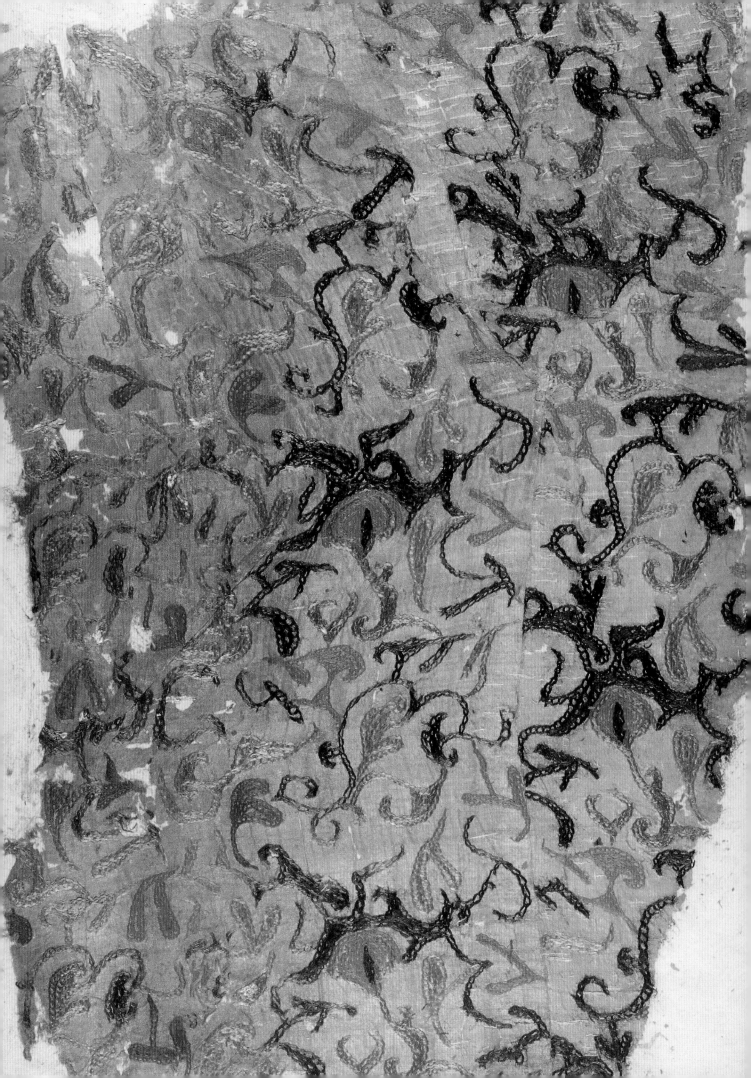

135. Colored printed gauze

136. Embroidery with longevity pattern on yellow thin, tough silk   Silk fabrics of Western Han, unearthed from a Han tomb at Mawangdui, Changsha, Hunan Province, in 1972. The textile industry was well developed in the Western Han, especially the silk industry, whose advanced techniques made possible a much larger output, more kinds and categories, and more variation in design. Production by state-run silk workshops was on a very large scale. The exquisite silk fabrics they turned out not only satisfied domestic needs but were sold to foreign markets far away, providing the material base for trade and prosperity along the Silk Road that spanned the Eurasian continent. Most of the varieties of Han fabrics that are already known can be found among the "riding the clouds" embroidery on yellowish brown silk and other fabrics unearthed from the Han tomb at Mawangdui, Changsha. They are complete in color spectrum, brilliant and sophisticated in design, exquisite in workmanship; rare treasures among excavated cultural relics that fully demonstrated the high technical level of silk weaving in the Han Dynasty.

135

136

137. Painted pottery jar with blue-dragon, white-tiger and scarlet-bird designs Burial object of Xin, Wang Mang's regime, height 48.5 cm, mouth diameter 18.8 cm, base diameter 18.1 cm; unearthed from a Han tomb at Shaogou, Luoyang, Henan Province, in 1953. Gray pottery was the principal member of the pottery family of the Han Dynasty. Vessels of this kind are generally bluish gray. The duration and degree of firing was even, the temperature being a little above 1000°C. The finished products were very hard and some were painted with color designs after firing but the paints peeled off easily. They were called painted pottery and were used especially as burial objects. The pottery jar shown here is an example. Its patterns of blue dragons, white tigers and scarlet birds are brightly colored and exquisitely wrought.

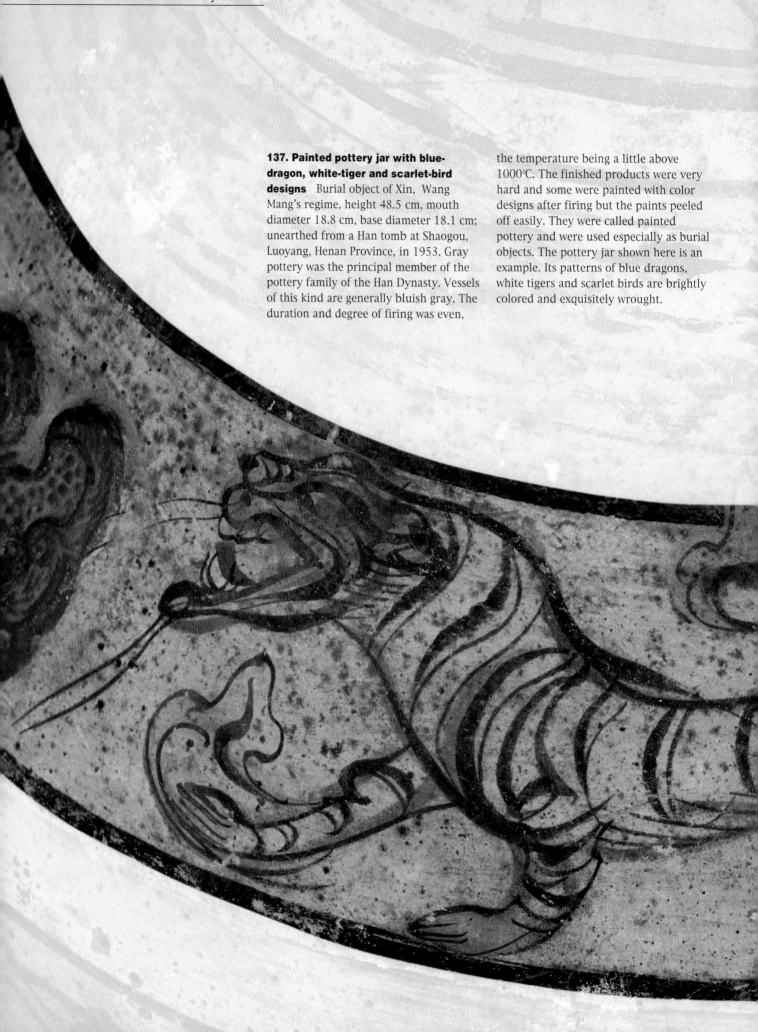

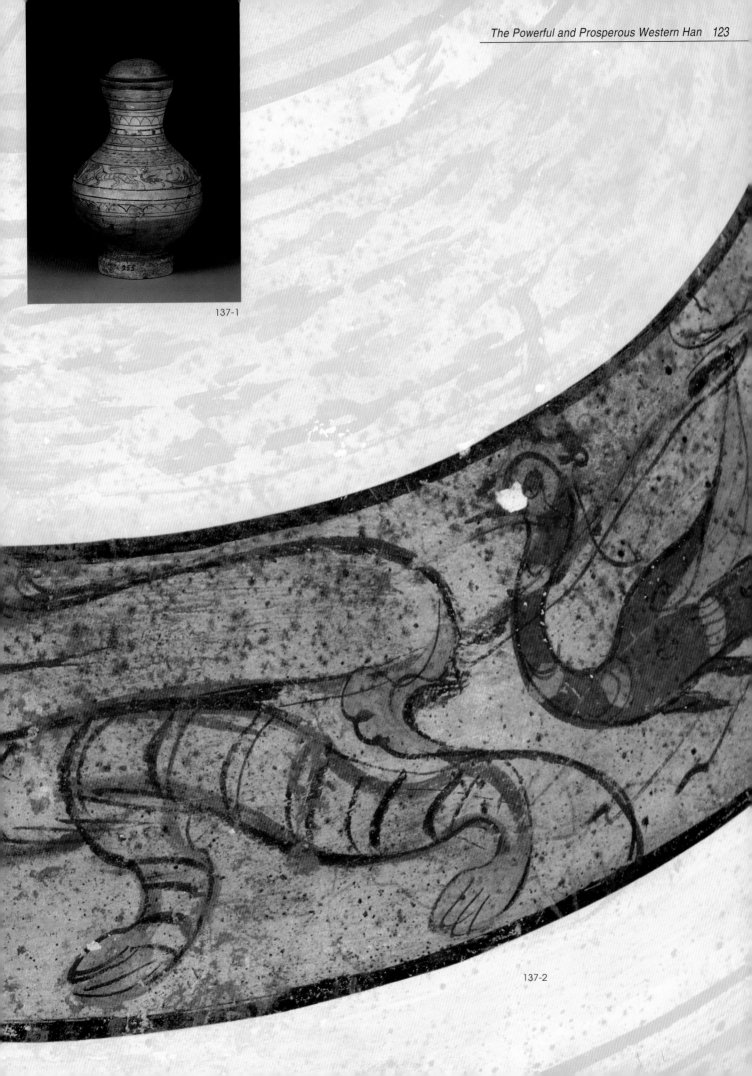

137-1

137-2

138. Glazed pottery jar with animal designs in relief Burial object of Western Han, height 31.7 cm, mouth diameter 12.8 cm, base diameter 12.8 cm. Glazed pottery was a new invention of the pottery-making industry of the Han Dynasty. It was made by firing ordinary clay. It had a red body, on which a layer of lead glaze was applied, which could be yellow, yellowish brown or green in color. The firing temperature was about 800℃. Such vessels were popular in the Yellow River Valley and other northern areas; they were also called northern glazed pottery. As the pottery was not hard, and the glaze peeled off or deteriorated easily, they were used mainly as burial objects. The glazed jar shown here is a good example of glazed pottery. On the upper part of the belly are animal designs in relief.

138-1

138-2

139-1

139. Green-glazed hard pottery *bu* with two beast-design ears Water or wine container, Western Han, height 21 cm, mouth diameter 12.1 cm, bottom diameter 15.6 cm; unearthed in Ningbo, Zhejiang Province, in 1955. In the Han Dynasty, hard pottery was widely used in south China. Preserving the lingering remnants of the so-called "hard pottery with impressed geometric design" of the late Neolithic Age, it formed its own style among the pottery of the Han Dynasty. Some Han earthernware were coated with yellow and green glaze and closely resembled porcelain. On the body of the *bu* shown here are three circles of bow-string designs, with ripple patterns in between. Coated with green and yellow glaze, this *bu* is a typical southern hard pottery of Western Han.

139-2

140

140. Ripple-pattern green-glazed hard pottery *hu* with two rings Wine or water container of Western Han, height 21.2 cm, mouth diameter 9 cm, bottom diameter 10 cm; unearthed at Yuquan, Hangzhou, Zhejiang Province, in 1957. In the Han Dynasty, glazed hard pottery vessels were widely used in places south of the Yangtze River, including present-day Guangdong, Guangxi, Hunan, Jiangxi, Fujian, Zhejiang and southern Jiangsu. They were made of thick and sticky clay obtained locally, which had to be fired at a temperature higher than that for gray pottery and had a harder texture. Sometimes a thin layer of yellow or green glaze was coated on the surface and this, too, had to be heated at a high temperature. Such glazed ware belonged to the green glaze family. On the neck of the pottery *hu* shown here is a ring of incised ripple patterns; on its belly are two circles of bow-string patterns in relief. Its body is coated with green and yellow glaze. The *hu* is a typical southern glazed hard pottery of Western Han.

Commerce and Communication

Commerce and communication in the Western Han were well developed, so was overseas trade. Chang'an, the capital, and Luoyang, Wan, Linzi, Handan, Chengdu and Fanyu were commercial centers. Boats and ox-and horse-drawn carriages were the major means of communication.

141. Ancient vehicle made of wood and bamboo　Burial object of Western Han, 106 cm long; unearthed at Wujialing, Changsha, Hunan Province, in 1952. The government of Western Han repaired and extended the network of roads of the preceding Qin Dynasty, forming a nationwide water-and-land communication network with Chang'an at the center. It also improved the means of transportation, producing more and more varieties of vehicles, thus accelerating the circulation of commodities and promoting prosperity in commerce. This is a model of a vehicle similar to a small horse-drawn carriage in those days, though a bit simple and crude. It was usually used as a vehicle for two passengers.

141

Wang Mang's Reform; Downfall of Western Han

In the late Western Han, annexation of land by local despots was intensified, slavery and servitude increased sharply, and all society faced an increasingly severe crisis. In AD 8 Wang Mang, a relative of the imperial family, proclaimed himself emperor and established the Xin Dynasty to replace the Han. To extricate the country from its predicament, he carried out a number of reforms. He changed all private land into the "king's land" and prohibited the buying and selling of land and slaves. He also carried out currency reforms on several occasions, but failed each time. Peasant uprisings such as those of the Green Woodsmen, Red Eyebrows and Bronze Horses broke out in both northern and southern China and in AD 23 Wang Mang's short-lived Xin Dynasty was overthrown.

142. Bronze mirror bearing the inscription "Second Year of Shijianguo"
Relic of Xin Dynasty, diameter 16 cm, thickness 0.4 cm. Patterns on the back of mirrors became more sophisticated during the reign of Wang Mang. Some inscriptions on mirrors recorded the year in which they were made. The mirror shown here was made in a state-run workshop in the second year of Shijianguo (AD 10), the earliest year-recording mirror discovered in China. On the back is an inscription of 54 characters, expressing Wang Mang's wish for peace and stability in the country after he established the Xin Dynasty in place of the Han.

142-2

142-1

143. Coins used during Wang Mang's Xin Dynasty   In the last years of Western Han, Wang Mang, who held power in the country, tried to overcome the serious social crisis by carrying out currency reform. In the second year of Jushe (AD 7), in addition to the five-*zhu* coins in circulation, he ordered the mintage of new coins called *yidaoping* -5000, qidao-500 and *daquan*-50. After he founded the Xin Dynasty and made himself emperor, he withdrew from circulation the *yidaoping*-5000 and *qidao*-500 as well as the Han five-*zhu* coins in the first year of his reign

titled Shijianguo (AD 9). In place of the five-*zhu* coins he issued new ones called *xiaoquanzhi*-one. Then in the second year of his reign (AD 10) he adopted a *baohuo* currency system with 28 varieties of money. In between the *daquan*-50 and *xiaoquanzhi*-one were four denominations known as the *zhuangquan*-40, *zhongquan*-30, *youquan*-20 and *yaoquan*-10 respectively. Collectively they were called the six varieties of *quan* currency (see the six coins in top row of photo). In the first year of his reign titled Tianfeng (AD 14) Wang Mang carried out a fourth currency

reform, changing to the use of *huobu* and *huoquan* coins. Finally, in the second year of Dihuang (AD 21), he ordered the mintage of coins called *buquan*. These currency reforms did not resolve the social contradictions of his time. On the contrary, they worsened the financial and monetary situation. But the coins Wang Mang minted were exquisite works of art; they are among the finest examples of ancient coins. The calligraphy of the inscriptions on them was superb and some inscriptions were inlaid with gold.

144. Coin with inscription "Guo Bao Jin Kui Zhi Wan" Currency of the Xin Dynasty, length 6.2 cm, weight 41.7 grams. The upper part of the coin is round with a square hole in the center. Four characters "Guo Bao Jin Kui "(national treasure)were cast on the four sides of the hole. The lower part of the coin is a square, on which are the two characters "Zhi Wan" (worth 10,000 *qian* of gold). It was probably used along with the ten varieties of *buhuo*. However, as the ten varieties of *buhuo* were withdrawn from circulation in less than a year, the coin shown here may have never been circulated officially, which is why it has not been found anywhere, except for a few pieces unearthed in and around Han City in present-day Xi'an. In the Han Dynasty one catty of gold was worth 10,000 *qian* (a traditional unit of weight,equivalent to 0.01 catty), so this coin represented one catty of gold and was the equivalent of a gold coin. During Wang Mang's regime, the circulation of gold was strictly prohibited and all persons from dukes and princes to the common people were forbidden to carry gold with them. This coin may have been cast as a substitute for the gold coin. Though covered with green rust, it was well cast and well preserved, and is a rare treasure among ancient coins.

144

145. Copper mother mold for casting the coin *dabuhuangqian* Xin Dynasty, 9.1 cm long, 7.4 cm wide. In the second year of Shijianguo (AD 10), Wang Mang carried out a third currency reform, adopting the *baohuo* system of 28 varieties, which included six varieties of *quanhuo*, five varieties of *beihuo*, four varieties of *guibao* and 10 varieties of *buhuo*. The *dabuhuangqian* was one of the 10 varieties of *buhuo*. The third currency reform caused great confusion and aroused vehement opposition from the people, who continued to use five-*zhu*

coins privately. Wang Mang then issued orders prohibiting the use of five-*zhu* coins and severely punishing those who used them. When countless people ranging from high officials to common people were found violating his orders, Wang Mang was forced to abolish the *baohuo* system the same year, but the *xiaoquanzhi*-one and *daquan*-50 remained in circulation. The copper mother mold for casting the *dabuhuangqian* shown here has provided material for the study of coin casting in the Han Dynasty. It is also a relic of Wang Mang's short-lived third currency reform.

146. Pottery mold of *Daquan*-50 Mold for casting coins of the Xin Dynasty, unearthed in 1958 at the site of a kiln making coin molds during Wang Mang's regime on the northwestern outskirts of Xi'an, Shaanxi Province. *Daquan*-50 was first minted in the second year of Jushe (AD 7). It was one of the new coins of Wang Mang's first currency reform. After Wang's fourth currency reform in the first year of Tianfeng (AD 14),this coin, though still used, rapidly devaluated. Finally, in the first year of Dihuang (AD 20), its circulation was banned. But the *daquan*-50 was in use for quite a long time and the mold shown here is evidence of this fact.

145

146

147

147.Bronze *hu*   A weight of the Xin Dynasty, height 26.1 cm, mouth diameter 32.8 cm; said to have been unearthed in Zhongmou County, Henan Province. The body of the *hu* bears an inscription of 81 characters in seal script, recording the promulgation nationwide of standard weights and measures by Wang Mang.

148. Bronze ring-shaped *quan*   A weight of the Xin Dynasty, outer ring diameter 28.05 cm, hole diameter 9.6 cm, weight 29.95 kg; unearthed at Chenggouyi, Dingxi County, Gansu Province, in 1927. This weight was cast in the first year of Shijianguo(AD 9). Based on figures given in the inscription on it, one catty in those days was the equivalent of 249.6 grams.

148-1

148-2

149. Bronze square *dou* A dry measure for grain of the Xin Dynasty, total length 23.92 cm, height 11 cm, volume 1,940 ml. On the upper and lower edges of the *dou* are lacquer paintings of millet, wheat, beans and hemp. The inscriptions tell that the vessel was cast in the first year of Shijianguo (AD 9) of Wang Mang's regime. The standard ruler used during Wang Mang's reign was 23.05 cm long, approximately the same as the ruler (23.2 cm) used by Shang Yang of Qin in the Warring States Period. One *sheng* during Wang Mang's time was equivalent to 16.2 cubic *cun*, which was the same as the cubic *sheng* used by Shang Yang of Qin. Thus after China was unified under the Qin Dynasty, the country's system of weights and measures remained stable for a relatively long period.

149-1

149-2

Expansion of Despotic Forces in Eastern Han

After the fall of the Xin Dynasty Liu Xiu, a member of the Han royal family re-established the Han Dynasty in AD 25. He established his capital at Luoyang, to the east of the former Western Han's capital Xi'an, and his dynasty was known as the Eastern Han in history. Meanwhile, landlords continued to expand their power and influence. They manipulated the government at all levels and obtained control over extensive portions of the country's farmland. Political corruption in the late Eastern Han resulted in numerous peasant uprisings. In AD 184 a large-scale rebellion known as the Uprising of the Yellow Turbans broke out, which seriously undermined the rule of the Eastern Han Dynasty.

Political Rule of Rich and Powerful Clans

The Eastern Han imperial court represented the interests of the newly emerging landlords. Rich and powerful clans often held high official posts from generation to generation. They had large numbers of "disciples," loyal onetime subordinates and private armies, and effectively controlled the political power of the central and local governments.

150. Green-glazed pottery model of a tower-pavilion Burial object of Eastern Han, 144 cm tall; unearthed at Guhe, Gaotang County, Shandong Province, in 1956. From the Eastern Han Dynasty on, construction of tall buildings gradually decreased except when there was some special need, but wooden towers increased noticeably. By rational use of architectural techniques, such wooden structures could provide shade from the sun, keep off the rain, and permit a person to enjoy leisurely a distant view. The eaves and platform on each floor protruded and contracted in a rhythmic way, giving the tower a stable but varying appearance with a contrast between light and shade, concrete and abstract. Such towers are models of China's ancient wooden buildings, examples that have been followed for a long time. The pottery tower-pavilion shown here is a typical wooden building of those far away times.

151. Pottery figure of a *buqu*, a landlord's soldier Burial object of Eastern Han, 38.8 cm tall; unearthed from a cliffside grave in Sichuan Province. In the Eastern Han, powerful landlords had their own manors. They forced tenant farmers to engage in productive labor for them, and kept some farmers under arms as soldiers in their private army. In the event of an emergency, these soldiers would be required to defend the manors. The figure shown here is a realistic portrayal of such a soldier.

150

151

152-1

152. Pottery courtyard Burial object of Eastern Han, 41.2 cm long, 40 cm wide, 29.6 cm high; unearthed at Mayinggang, eastern suburbs of Guangzhou, Guangdong Province, in 1956. This is a model of a square courtyard with watchtowers commanding distant views. It shows warriors carrying weapons, the master sitting upright at a small table, and laborers kneeling subserviently. It is a true reflection of the power of despotic landlords of the Eastern Han, whose homes had to be well-fortified castles because of the class antagonism and social unrest in those days.

152-2

Social Economy and Feudal Country Estates

The Eastern Han period saw continued development of the social economy. Ox-plowing was further popularized, iron farm tools were widely used, and water conservancy was intensified. Iron-smelting and handicraft production such as pottery and porcelain all made new progress. The greatest progress was made in the south. Despotic landlords occupied large tracts of land and controlled large numbers of dependent peasants and slaves. In general, they went in for agriculture on their manors and concurrently engaged in animal husbandry, handicraft and commerce, practicing a more or less self-sufficient economy.

153. Iron scythe Farm tool of Eastern Han, distance between two ends 56.5 cm; unearthed at Mumashan, Xinjin County, Sichuan Province, in 1957. This is a big scythe. When used, a wooden handle was inserted into one end and the user held it with both hands to cut weeds or crops. As the scythe had a wide reach, it could work fast and was especially suitable for harvesting widely sown crops and forage grass.

154. Rubbing of a stone engraving of ox-drawn plowing (section) A piece of decoration in a tomb chamber, 82.6 cm

high and 105.5 cm wide; unearthed from an Eastern Han tomb at Shuanggouzhen, Suining County, Jiangsu Province, in 1952. Before the Qin and Han dynasties, plowing was done by human labor alone; ox-

plowing did not play a major rule until the Western Han when it was introduced extensively and became popular in the Central Plains. During the Eastern Han, ox-plowing was introduced gradually to the Yangtze and Pearl River valleys. The *History of the Later Han Dynasty* contains many accounts of the meritorous deeds of county magistrates and prefects in remote areas, who taught and encouraged local officials and people to plow with the ox. This stone engraving shows a plow drawn by two oxen at work south of the Yangtze.

153

154

155. Remnant of a pottery figure with a hoe Eastern Han burial object, unearthed at Qinggangpo, Chengdu, Sichuan Province, in 1952; height of remnant 20 cm. Weeding with hoes was a top priority during mid-term tillage. The *Book of Fan Shengzhi* repeatedly mentioned the need for "early hoeing," "frequent hoeing" and "hoeing whenever the grass grows not minding the trouble," so evidently hoeing was important to the raising of crops. In the Han Dynasty some hoes were made entirely of iron; the blade was flat with two sloping shoulders or shaped like a trapezoid. Some hoes were made of wood and had an iron blade. The hoe held by this incomplete pottery figure is a wooden one with an iron blade.

156. Pottery figure of farmer with a spade Eastern Han burial object, height 20.5 cm; unearthed at Laodaosi, Mian County, Shaanxi Province, in 1978. Spades of the Han Dynasty evolved from primitive plow-like farm tools and were used for deep plowing. They were also used in earthwork like dredging a river, building earth terraces or walls. The *History of the Han Dynasty* contains scenes of laborers digging canals and ditches with spades. It also contains the phrase "chest load", which means using a spade to load a large box with mud to be carried away. The spade with an iron blade and wooden handle shown here is a typical tool of the Han Dynasty.

155

157. Stone picture in Wang Deyuan's tomb   Decoration inside a tomb chamber, Eastern Han; unearthed in Suide County, Shaanxi Province, in 1953. The appearance of large manors in various parts of the country was characteristic of the economic life of Eastern Han. Though agriculture was the main occupation, a manor economy included animal husbandry, cultivation of plants such as fruits, vegetables, mulberry and hemp, boiling salt, brewing wine, and many

kinds of handicrafts. The larger manors were self-sufficient. Their owners had all they needed and administered their estate like an independent kingdom. The stone picture here shows food crops, herds of cattle and sheep, horse-drawn vehicles, oxen tilling the land, rare birds and beasts, as well as amusements at banquets, singing and dancing, outings, etc. It reflects the work and life styles of powerful landlords in northern Shaanxi.

157

158. Brick relief with scene of people husking rice   Relic of Eastern Han, decoration in a tomb chamber, 25 cm tall, 39 cm wide; unearthed in Pengshan County, Sichuan Province, in 1955. Cereal processing saw new advances in the Han Dynasty. In addition to the pestle and mortar, use of which started before the Qin Dynasty, there appeared the treadle-operated tilt hammer and tilt hammers pulled by draught animals or operated by hydraulic power. Labor intensity gradually lessened while work efficiency was raised. The treadle-operated tilt hammer was especially popular. Huan Tan, a philosopher of the late Western Han, said that using the treadle-operated tilt hammer was ten times faster than husking by hand. This brick carving depicts the structure of the treadle-operated tilt hammer and how it works.

159. Stone model of paddy field and pond   Eastern Han burial object, length 81 cm, width 48 cm, height 11 cm; unearthed at Shuangfuxiang, Emei County, Sichuan Province, in 1979. This stone model of a paddy field and pond consists of two parts. On the left are two paddy plots, one containing piles of fertilizer, the other showing two farmers with backs bent working the plot. On the right is a pond, in which are a small boat, a turtle, a frog, river snails, lotus seedpots, etc. It is a model of a pondside paddy field in the Han Dynasty. Making extensive use of small riverside ponds was a form of water conservancy in the Han Dynasty. The ponds were used to store water for irrigation, breed fish and grow lotus, measures that helped develop diversified agricultural production. The Eastern Han government appointed officials to take charge of riverside ponds and promote their development. Owners of large manors also paid attention to the building of such ponds. Their appearance all over south China reflected improvement in water conservancy techniques.

158

159

160. Pottery *cang* (granary) Eastern Han burial object, height 77 cm; unearthed in Xingyang County, Henan Province, in 1958. The *cang* and *lin* were buildings used to store grain. A *cang* was a storehouse for unhusked grain while a *lin* was used to keep husked rice. Therefore a *cang* was generally larger than a *lin*. For better ventilation and to avoid dampness, the floor of a *cang* was usually built higher than the ground outside and it was reached by means of a flight of steps. Under the corbel brackets were windows. Some *cang* were intricately designed: they had wooden floors, under which were holes for air. These holes, together with the windows near the roof, provided better ventilation. The model pottery *cang* shown here is a two-story one, with a flat seat between the stories. The upper story has five windows. Above and below the flat seat are murals depicting activities relating to storing grain.

160

161. Brick relief of harvesting, fishing and hunting   Eastern Han tomb chamber decoration, height 36 cm, width 42 cm; unearthed at Yangzishan, Chengdu, Sichuan Province, in 1954. This brick relief consists of two parts. The upper part is a scene of hunters shooting at birds with arrows to which silk sashes are tied. Tied to the lower end of the arrow is a small movable stone called *bo.* In the picture this stone is placed in a semicircular device. The lower part portrays a harvesting scene in a paddy field. There are three persons on the left, each holding a sickle in one hand to cut the crops. Two persons on the right are removing the stalks with scythes. The scenes are realistic depictions of harvesting, fishing and hunting in those days.

161

162. Color-glazed pottery chicken coop
Eastern Han burial object, height 15cm;
unearthed in Changsha, Hunan Province.
Chicken and pigs were the main animals raised
for meat in many parts of the country in the
Han Dynasty. They were usually raised in pens
and coops on a small scale. Nevertheless, they
were the chief source of meat. The pottery coop
shown here is an example of domestic raising of
chickens in the Eastern Han.

163. Pottery pigpen   Eastern Han burial object,
height 15.5 cm; unearthed in Changsha, Hunan
Province. Raising pigs not only provides meat
but is an important source of fertilizers in
agriculture. To raise pigs and collect manure,

162

various kinds of pigpens were designed and
built in ancient China. During the Han Dynasty,
there were detached pens and pens coupled to
latrines or workshops. The pen-and-latrine
shown here was popular in China's farm areas
over a very long period, especially in the north.
It played a significant role in the development
of agricultural production in ancient times.

163

164

164. Brick relief of a brewery
Eastern Han tomb chamber
decoration, height 28.4 cm, width
38.3 cm; unearthed in Peng County,
Sichuan Province, in 1954. Wine
brewing was a large-scale handicraft
industry in the Western and Eastern
Han dynasties. Wineshops and
breweries could be found in almost
every city and town. The scene
depicted here shows urn-shaped wine
vessels for brewing,wine for sale in a
big jar, sellers and buyers, and a
worker ready to deliver the wine. It is
a revealing scene of wine production
and sale in a small wineshop and
brewery, a reflection of the
popularity of drinking and the
prosperity of the wine-brewing
industry in Sichuan Province during
the Han Dynasty.

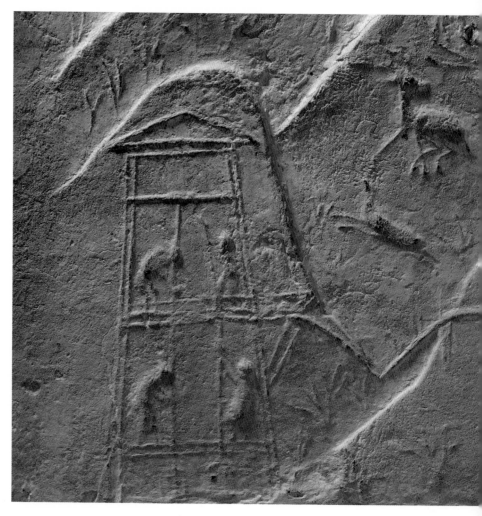

165-1

166

165-2

165. Brick relief of a saltern

Eastern Han tomb chamber decoration, height 41.2 cm, width 46.5 cm, thickness 6 cm; unearthed at Yangzishan, Chengdu, Sichuan Province, in 1954. The salt industry developed rapidly in the Eastern Han, during which areas producing salt were widespread. In Sichuan and Yunnan provinces, well salt was the main product. This scene depicts the whole process of extracting and producing salt. A high derrick with a pulley and bucket was set up to collect the brine. The derrick had two stories, and on each story were two persons facing each other collecting the brine with a pulley-tackle. The brine was then conducted across a mountain stream by means of a long bamboo conduit, from which it flowed into a jar. Finally, it was poured into a big pot and boiled slowly. Collecting and boiling the brine were two closely connected processes.

166. Brick relief of a tung orchard

Eastern Han tomb chamber decoration, height 24.2 cm, width 37.4 cm; unearthed in Pengshan County, Sichuan Province, in 1954. People in the Han Dynasty used tung oil for lighting. Tung oil was a special product of southwest China; and planting tung trees and extracting oil from tung seeds was a major sideline on local manors. This relief shows an aspect of the self-sufficient manor economy of Eastern Han.

167-1

167-2

167. Iron *shu*-knife (knife-pen) with gold inlay Eastern Han relic, length 18.5 cm, width 1.5 cm; unearthed at Tianhuishan, Chengdu, Sichuan Province, in 1957. Before China invented paper, people used bamboo slips to write on. When writing on such slips, the writer needed a small knife to trim the slips. It was called a *shu*-knife (knife-pen) in the Han Dynasty. At first, such knives were made of bronze; later iron was used. Most *shu*-knives of the Han Dynasty were made of iron. By the Eastern Han they had become important articles that people would carry on their person. The most famous knife-pen at the time was called the "gold-horse"; it bore a gold-inlaid horse pattern with the name of the engraver. "Gold-horse" knife-pens were made by craftsmen hired by the government of Guanghan Prefecture, Sichuan Province. The one shown here was also made by them, but the gold-inlaid pattern is not of a horse, but of a bird.

167-3

168

168. Rubbing from stone carving, depicting a scene of iron smelting

Eastern Han tomb chamber decoration, height of stone surface 80 cm, width 144 cm; unearthed in Teng County, Shandong Province, in 1930. Beginning in the reign of Emperor Wu of Western Han, the Han government set up 49 public iron offices in different parts of the country and forbade private industrial and commercial magnates to engage in iron smelting. It was not until the reign of Emperor He of Eastern Han that the ban was lifted. This picture depicts a scene of iron smelting by a powerful clan after the lifting of the ban. The people on the left are using multipipe air blasting bags; they are forging iron weapons.

169. Steel knife Eastern Han weapon, length 111.5 cm; unearthed in Cangshan County, Shandong Province, in 1974. Great progress was made in steel-manufacturing during the Western and Eastern Han dynasties. A new technique called *chaogang* (literally "frying steel") appeared, which was to heat pig iron mixed with ore powder to reduce the carbon content; then to forge steel parts with this low-carbon iron as raw material. The steel knife shown here was probably made of such material, which was subjected to repeated folding and forging that produced a dense texture and even composition with less foreign material, thus upgrading the quality of the product. An inscription on the knife indicated it had been heated, folded and forged 30 times.

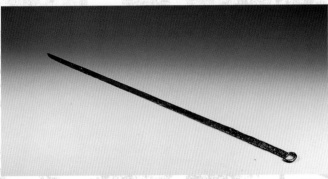

169-1

169-2

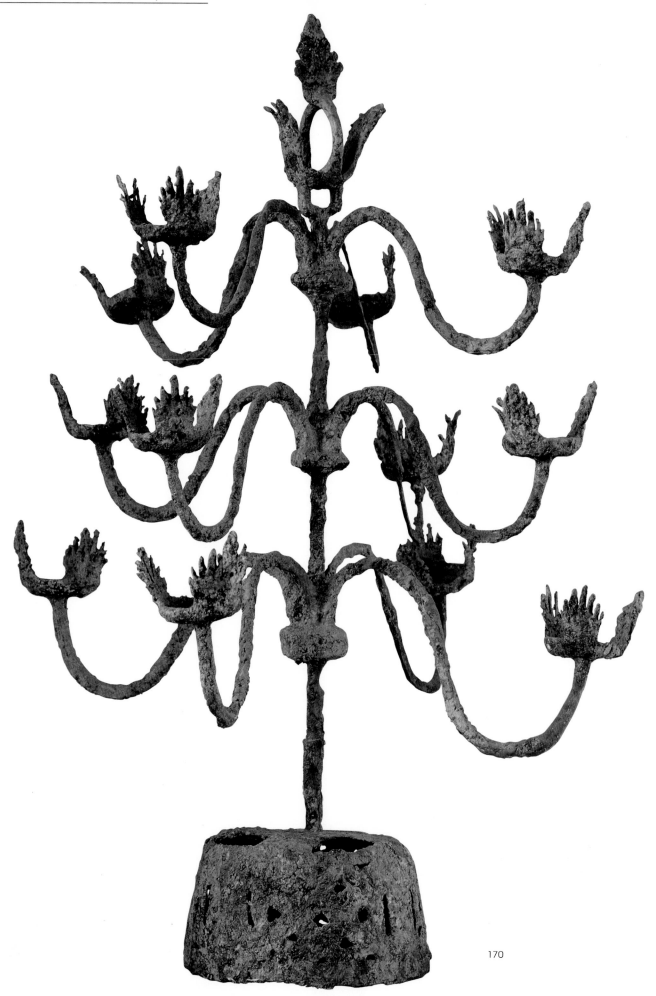

170

171

170. Iron oil lamp with 12 disks Lighting device of Eastern Han, 73 cm tall; unearthed in Shaogou, Luoyang, Henan Province, in 1953. This lamp, shaped like a tree bearing blossoms, is one of many varieties of oil lamps used in the Han Dynasty. The lamp post is like a trunk with branches arranged symmetrically. At the top of each branch is a disk for holding a wick or the figure of a scarlet-bird. People named such lamps by the number of disks they held: 5-disk lamp, 7-disk lamp, 12-disk lamp,13-disk lamp and 15-disk lamp. Usually such a lamp is about one meter high. The 12-disk lamp shown here was exquisitely made and beautifully decorated. It must have belonged to a rich family.

171. Iron mirror with gold-inlaid five-animal design Relic of Eastern Han, diameter 16.5 cm, edge thickness 0.8 cm. This iron mirror bears the images of five animals inlaid with gold filigree. Cao Cao in his *Miscellaneous Imperial Household Articles* records that the emperor used a 1.2 *chi* (a *chi* is a traditional unit of length about 0.33 meter) iron mirror with gold inlay and the empress and crown prince used four iron mirrors with silver inlay. The technique of making iron mirrors with gold or silver inlay was not well developed until the end of the Han Dynasty.

172. Rubbing from a stone engraving of silk weavers   Tomb chamber decoration of Eastern Han, height of stone surface 99 cm, width 234 cm; unearthed at Honglou Village, Tongshan County, Xuzhou, Jiangsu Province, in 1956. The picture shows the three steps in silk weaving of the Han Dynasty: First, twisting; the woman on the right is twisting silk with a twister. Second, interlacing; the woman in the middle is interlacing the horizontal silk threads with a weft wheel. Third, loom weaving. The textile industry was fairly well developed in what is now Sichuan and Shandong provinces during the Han Dynasty, Shandong being most famous for its silk fabrics. This stone picture is of a weaving scene in a despotic landlord's house in Shandong Province during the Eastern Han.

173

173. Green-glazed pottery ewer Wine or grain container of Eastern Han, height 47 cm; unearthed in Wei County, Shandong Province. Glazed soft pottery first appeared in the Guanzhong area (Shaanxi Province) during the mid-Western Han. It was usually fired at a temperature of about 700°-800℃. Glaze in green or yellowish brown was very common, but there were also multi-colored glazes of yellow, green and reddish brown. During the late Western Han and early Eastern Han, glazed soft pottery was widely used in the Yellow River valley and other places in the north; it also appeared in the Yangtze River valley. The green-glazed pottery ewer shown here is a typical northern product of the Eastern Han.

174

174. Four-handled celadon jar   Container of Eastern Han, height 16.5 cm, belly diameter 18.5 cm; unearthed at Zhong-zhou Road, Luoyang, Henan Province, in 1955. The sides of the mouth are straight; the belly is round; and the base is flat. On the upper part of each of the four sides of the belly is a half-ring ear, to which a string can be tied. The jar is pale gray; the glaze on it is thin and even, but with some hacks. Between the shoulder and belly is a line like a bow string. The belly is decorated with rhomboid patterns. Kaolin was used as raw material. It was baked at a very high temperature, producing a hard body. Judging from the shape of the jar, it must be a product of the middle or lower reaches of the Yangtze River. It is a typical celadon vessel of the late Eastern Han.

175. Celadon *bu* Wine or water container of Eastern Han, height 23.6cm, mouth diameter 20.8 cm; unearthed at Baijiazhen, Shangyu County, Zhejiang Province. The Shangyu area of Zhejiang was where the technique of making celadonware developed from primitive stage to maturity. During the mid-and late Eastern Han, matured celadonware was made in both Shangyu and Ningbo of Zhejiang, and also in Yongjia in the southern part of the province. This laid the foundation for the famous Yue kiln of the Tang Dynasty.

175

176

176. Celadon *zhan* Food vessel of Eastern Han, height 9.1 cm, mouth diameter 17.2 cm; unearthed in Changsha, Hunan Province. Celadon was made of white clay, glazed all over and fired at a high temperature of about 1,300℃. The celadon *zhan* shown here is coated with a glaze that is bright and pure. When struck, the vessel emits a clear sound. It is an example of the quality of celadonware of the Eastern Han period.

177. Painted bone ruler and gilded bronze ruler Linear measures of Eastern Han, length 22.9 cm and 23.6 cm respectively; the former was unearthed in Guyuan, Ningxia Hui Autonomous Region and the latter in Ye County, Shandong Province. The Han Dynasty retained the system of measures of previous dynasties. In general, the basic units of measure were based on certain parts of the human body, so it was hard to make them accurate. At one time the *jishu* (a cereal grass) was used as a standard of measure. But by the time of the great historian Sima Qian at the latest, a new method using the pitch-pipes called *lüguan* of ancient Chinese musical instruments had been invented. It used the *huangzhong* pipe (the pipe that emitted the first tone of the Chinese five-tone scale) as the basic unit and defined the interrelations of length, volume and weight by the length (one *chi*) and cross section (9 square *fen*) of this pipe. One *chi* of the Han Dynasty was equivalent to 23.08864 cm. It was divided into 9 *cun*, and each *cun* into 9 *fen*. An Eastern Han *chi* was a bit longer, but in general there were no appreciable changes in length of the *chi* during the Han Dynasty.

178. Brick engraving of a market scene
Tomb chamber decoration of Eastern Han, height 28 cm, width 48 cm; unearthed in Guanghan County, Sichuan Province. The engraving shows shops in a county market and people buying and selling. In those days markets could only be set up in certain parts of a city. They were surrounded by walls separating them from residential areas. A market had only one gate, through which people could enter and leave only during fixed hours. The three characters in the upper left corner of the brick picture read "East Market Gate". A county market of the Han Dynasty was administered by an official appointed by the county government; he was called the market chief and his office was in the market tower. Each day when the market opened a flag would be hoisted on top of the tower, and when it closed the flag would be lowered, so the tower was also called the flag-tower. It was the highest building in the area, from where all activities in the market lanes could be monitored. A drum hung in the tower sounded when the market opened or closed each day.

178

Life of the Rich and Powerful Clans

With the development of the economy and culture, the rich and powerful landlords of Eastern Han became increasingly extravagant in their food, clothing, housing and transportation, and indulged more and more in music and women.

179. Brocade shoe Relic of Eastern Han, length 23.2 cm, width 7.5 cm; unearthed from among the ruins of Loulan, Xinjiang Uygur Autonomous Region, in 1934. Han brocade was a high quality twill woven with colored silk threads. There were three varieties: broche in two colors, three colors and multicolors. In the Western Han Dynasty brocade was produced mainly in Xiangyi, Chengliu Prefecture (Sui County, Henan). Sichuan brocade was not well known until the late Eastern Han. Because of the damp climate in the Central Plains, articles of brocade were seldom found among the ruins or in the tombs there, but in Xinjiang where the climate was dry brocade articles have been unearthed frequently. Brocade of the Han Dynasty was sold to places as far away as Rome. The brocade shoe shown here was a high-quality footwear made in the interior of China. Unearthed in Xinjiang, it is material evidence that the Eurasian continent was already linked by the famous Silk Road at that time.

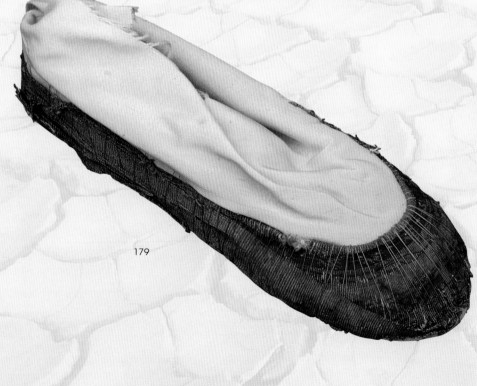

179

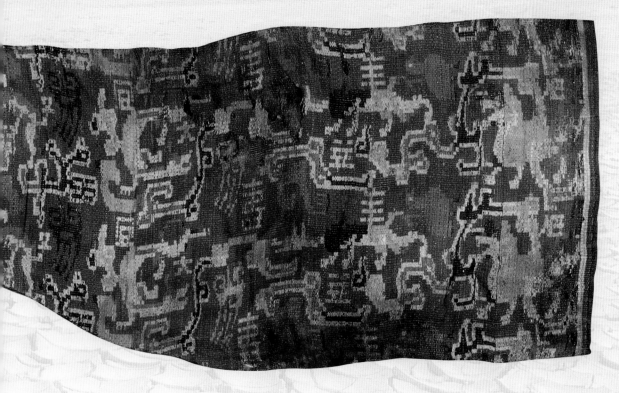

180

180. Brocade sock Relic of Eastern Han, length 43.5 cm, width 17.3 cm; unearthed at Niya, Minfeng County, Xinjiang Uygur Autonomous Region, in 1959. The sock was found on the foot of a male corpse. It was made of brocade intricately woven with colored silk threads, a kind of brocade that was called "prolonging life and benefiting one's sons and grandsons." The warp and weft crisscrossed in cycles like a jacquard weave. The loom used was the most advanced in the world in those days.

181. Embroidered perfume bag with colored cloud design Dress adornment of Eastern Han, length 7.5 cm; unearthed from the ruins of Loulan, Lop Nur, in Xinjiang Uygur Autonomous Region, in 1934. As embroidery requires much more labor than brocade weaving, it is more valuable than the latter. Embroidery techniques were highly advanced in the Han Dynasty, and embroidery workers when doing needlework often made appropriate improvements on the background design. The themes of embroidered works were varied. The perfume bag shown here is ornamented with flower and variant cloud patterns in red, yellow and green silk threads, embroidered on eaglewood-colored silk and cotton fabric. The needlework is in large rope, but the stitches are neat. At the edges of the designs, the needlework is in dense spirals with no blank space. A work of such quality shows that embroidery skills had attained maturity by this time.

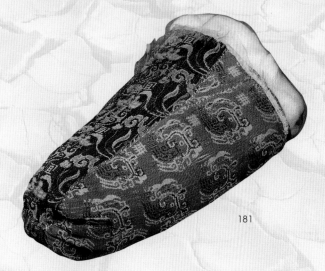

181

182. Horseshoe lacquer box Dressing box of Eastern Han, height 5.5 cm, length 8 cm, width 5.5 cm; unearthed at Daiye Village, Laixi County, Shandong Province. In the Han Dynasty, lacquer articles of the highest quality were inlaid with metal such as gold, silver or bronze along the edges. The lid of this box is inlaid with four silver leaves and the upper and lower edges are plated with silver. The inside and outside walls of the box are painted with cloud patterns.

183. Brick relief of a kitchen A piece of decoration in a tomb chamber, Eastern Han, width 40 cm, height 25 cm. Pictures of kitchens have been discovered in Han tombs in many parts of China. The contents were more or less the same, the only difference being that some were more elaborate than others. These pictures show that in the Han Dynasty cooking methods in various parts of the country were basically the same. They also show that the principal ways of cooking meat were roasting, steaming and boiling and the most common kitchen utensils were stoves, caldrons and steamers.

183

184. Pottery stove Burial object of
Eastern Han, height 26 cm; unearthed at
Xianlie Road, eastern suburbs of
Guangzhou, Guangdong Province, in 1955.
Using pottery stoves as burial objects in
large and medium-sized tombs was a
common practice after the mid-Western
Han. Large numbers of pottery stoves have
been unearthed and they show that stoves
used in different parts of the country were
different in shape. The stoves unearthed
in Luoyang and its vicinity are
rectangular, so are called square stoves. A
stove had only one opening in the
Western Han, but had three or four in the
Eastern Han. In the Guanzhong area
before the mid-Eastern Han most stoves
were shaped like horseshoes and were
called round stoves; they became square
in the late Eastern Han. In Shaan County,
Henan Province,between Luoyang and
Guanzhong, both square and round stoves
were used. During the mid- and late
Western Han, stoves shaped like boats
were widely used south of the Yangtze
River, and in the late Eastern Han the hind
part of some boat-shaped stoves was
turned upwards like a ship's bow; this was
the prototype of stoves of the Northern
and Southern dynasties.

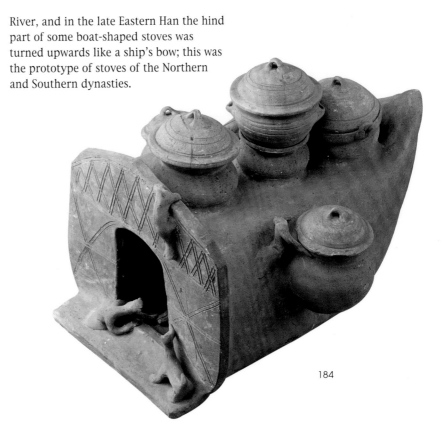

184

185. Rubbing from a stone engraving of a feast   Relic of Eastern Han, a piece of decoration in a tomb chamber; the stone engraving was unearthed in Yinan County, Shandong Province, in 1954. The left half of the engraving shows the grave occupant sitting on the floor. Beside him is a storehouse, piles of grain, and a vehicle for transporting grain. The right half contains a kitchen, a stove, a well and various utensils. It also shows people carrying a pig, slaughtering an ox and a sheep, boiling water, steaming rice, cooking, and preparing wine. The scene reflects the luxurious life of a rich and powerful family.

186. Pottery figurines of a maid and a cook   Burial objects of Eastern Han, height 38.5 cm and 38.3 cm respectively; unearthed in Hualongqiao, Chongqing, Sichuan Province, in 1957. During the Eastern Han rich and powerful families usually owned hundreds or thousands of slaves, and had control over many tenant peasants. The slaves had no personal freedom and were forced to do all kinds of heavy manual labor. The two figurines shown here are a cook and a maid, both slaves, serving food in a wealthy family.

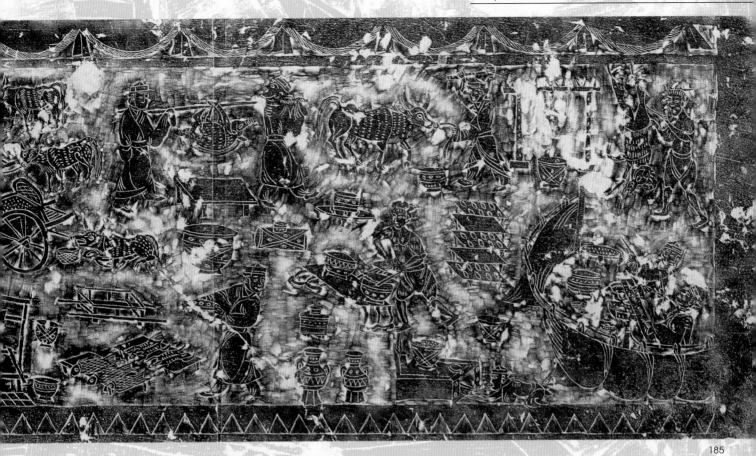

185

186

187. Green-glazed pottery water pavilion
Burial object of Eastern Han, height 54.5 cm; unearthed at Sanlixi Village, Xinzhuzhen, Xi'an, Shaanxi Province. The pavilion stands in the center of a simulated pool in a pottery basin, surrounded by figures of men, horses and geese. It is a two-storied structure, with a ladder on the lower floor for people to ascend to the upper floor. At the four corners of the balustrade on the upper floor are figures of warriors drawing bows. Inside the pavilion are figures dancing, playing the *qin* (a seven-string plucked instrument), and clapping hands to the accompaniment of singing. In the last years of the Eastern Han, rich and powerful families built castles and organized private armies. The warriors in the pottery water pavilion are landlord's soldiers, realistically portrayed.

188. Brick picture of a house with courtyards Decoration inside a tomb chamber of the Eastern Han, height 40 cm, width 46.5 cm, thickness 6.3 cm; unearthed at Yangzishan, Chengdu, Sichuan Province, in 1954. This is a fairly complete picture of a rich and powerful family's house with courtyards. The house, surrounded by high walls, is complete with halls and chambers, a kitchen and a well. In the inner courtyard two cranes are dancing and two chickens fighting. The host and his guest sit face to face in the hall drinking. The room behind the hall is a bedroom, which is not shown in the picture. A hall in front, a bedroom or bedrooms behind, kitchen in the east and toilet in the west—this is the standard type of dwelling house for officials and rich families at the time.

187

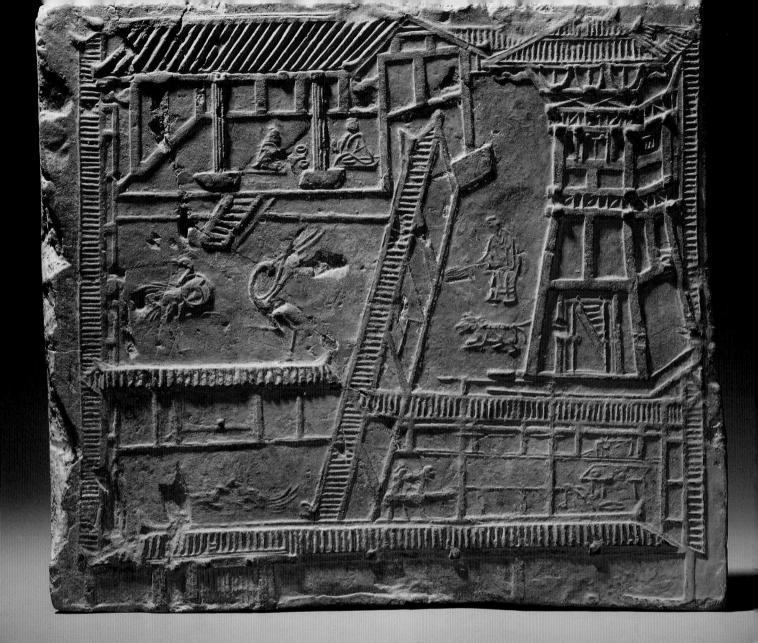

189. Three-in-one pottery house Burial object of
Eastern Han, length 31.6 cm, width 25.6 cm, height
23 cm; unearthed at Mayinggang, east suburbs of
Guangzhou, Guangdong Province, in 1957. The
three-in-one house structure was a type of
architecture of the Lingnan area in the Han
Dynasty. It consisted of three buildings joined
together like the Chinese character for concave
"凹". The front building, the largest, was
rectangular; the two rear buildings were symmetrical
and formed the wings. They were joined by a low
wall to enclose a backyard. On one or both sides of
the front building is a corridor, with a flight of steps
leading to the rear buildings. One of the rear
buildings contained a toilet; the other, pens for
livestock. Some of the pens opened on to the
courtyard. Most of the clay models of three-in-one
houses were unearthed from large brick tombs built
after the mid-Eastern Han; they were a reflection of
the social status of the tomb occupants.

189

190-1

190. Pottery boat   Burial object of Eastern Han, height 16 cm, length 54 cm; unearthed at Xianlie Road, Guangzhou, Guangdong Province, in 1954. On the prow of the boat is a heavy stone used as an anchor. The helm is in the back part of the boat; its shaft passes through the helmsman's cabin and is secured to the stern. The helm is different from that on modern river boats; it retains vestiges of the rudder from which it evolved. It is shorter than a rudder, but a bit longer than the helm of an ordinary river boat.

The helm was an important invention in boat-building technology in ancient China. The one shown here is the earliest so far discovered. There are six people on the boat, all in working postures. In proportion to the height of these figures, a real boat of this type would be 14-15 meters long with a loading capacity of more than 500 *hu* (a dry measure equal to 5-10 decalitre). On the deck are six groups of spears and shields, indicating that this is a model of an inland river boat with armed guards.

190-2

190-3

191. Brick picture of an ancient covered carriage

A decoration in a tomb chamber, Eastern Han, width 46.5 cm, height 39 cm, thickness 5.4 cm; unearthed at Yangzishan, Chengdu, Sichuan Province, in 1953. The cabin of a covered carriage in the Han Dynasty was a closed structure, with a window on each side and a door in the back. The top of the carriage was usually shaped like a canopy. The cabin consisted of two sections, front and rear. The master sat in the rear while the driver sat in front. Covered carriages were used mainly by women in the Han Dynasty. Records in many history books show that when the empress dowager, empress or imperial concubines went for an outing, they would ride in covered or curtained carriages. The brick picture shown here portrays some women of a rich family in a covered carriage.

192

192. Pottery model of a horse-drawn carriage Burial object of Eastern Han, length 17 cm, height 12.5 cm, horse height 15 cm; unearthed at Xianlie Road, Guangzhou, Guangdong Province, in 1955. There were many types of carriages in the Han Dynasty. The top of a horse-drawn carriage like this one was shaped like an awning. The entrance was in the rear. As such carriages were for women, the opening in front was covered with a curtain so that people outside could not see the passengers.

193. Brick with characters meaning "Blue Heaven has passed away" Tomb brick, length 37 cm, thickness 3 cm; unearthed at Yuanbaokeng Village, Bo County, Anhui Province, in 1976. This brick is from the wall of a tomb belonging to Cao Cao's ancestral clan. It bears 26 characters inscribed arbitrarily by a craftsman. "Blue Heaven" was a reference to the Eastern Han government and "Blue Heaven has passed away" was part of the slogan "Blue Heaven has passed away and it is time for Yellow Heaven to take over" put forward during the uprising of the Yellow Turbans. The Yellow Turbans were organized in line with the Doctrine of Peace, a Taoist sect, and their slogan was actually the call of this Taoist sect. The brick shown here reflects the widespread dissemination of the Doctrine on the eve of the uprising of the Yellow Turbans, as well as the wish of the people to overthrow the Han Dynasty.

Minority Nationalities During the Han Dynasty

The Western and Eastern Han dynasties were often referred to as the two Hans in history. During the two-Han period the unity of the country helped to strengthen ties and mutual influence between the Han and various minority peoples. Besides the populous Han nationality which resided mostly in the Central Plains, the principal minority nationalities in different parts of the country included the Xiongnu in the north, the Wuhuan and Xianbei in the northeast ,the Qiang in the northwest, various tribes in the Western Regions, Baiyue in the south and southeast, and the Southwestern Yi in the southwest. The people of all these nationalities created cultures of their own, contributing to the development of the multiethnic country.

194-1

Xiongnu Nationality

During the Han Dynasty, the Xiongnu in the north had a fairly well developed nomadic economy and grassland culture. Though occasional military conflicts occurred between the Han and the Xiongnu, over a relatively long period of time the two peoples carried on peaceful trade along the border and ties between them were friendly because of marriages of Han princesses to Xiongnu chieftains. During the reign of Emperor Yuan of Western Han, Chanyu Huhanxie, a Xiongnu chieftain, entered into an alliance with the Han court, pledging that "the Han and Xiongnu will merge into one family." Relics unearthed in areas where the Xiongnu people lived possess both the characteristics of grassland culture and the cultural style of the Han empire, confirming the close relations between the Han and Xiongnu.

194-2

194. Bronze seal with eight characters
Relic of Eastern Han, height 2.9 cm, length of each side 2.3 cm; unearthed at Upper Sunjiazhai, Datong County, Qinghai Province, in 1979. This was an official seal recording the allegiance of the Xiongnu chief Guiyi to the Han and was presented to the Xiongnu chief by the Eastern Han government according to a tradition established since the reign of Emperor Xuan of the Western Han. Usually a seal like this bore the character "Han," representing the Han Dynasty, the name of a tribe (a national minority), and a conferred title like Guiyi. The knob of the

seal was often shaped like a camel. The main body of the Xiongnu people had not yet moved into Qinghai Province in the Han Dynasty, but a branch called Lushuihu, whose origins were in Zhangye, Gansu Province, crossed the Qilian Mountain during the Eastern Han and settled among the Yuezhihu and Qiang tribes in the area of Huangzhong in eastern Qinghai. The name Xiongnu on the seal refers to this branch, Lushuihu.

195.Bronze buckle with figurines of three musicians   Ornament,4.5 cm long, 1.9 cm wide, Western Han; unearthed in 1956 in Jungar Banner, Inner Mongolia Autonomous Region. A buckle of this kind, known variously as *shibi*, *xianbei*, *xubi* or *xipi*, was an ornamental fastener for the leather belt worn by people of ancient Chinese ethnic minorities in the north. Diverse in shape, it curves at one end and has a round knob on the back. The popular costume of the Xiongnu, or the Huns, consisted of a jacket

195

196

197

buttoning down the front, long trousers, and a leather belt with a buckle. Tradition has it that the ornamental buckle was first used by the nomads on the northern grasslands and was not introduced into the Central Plains until the Spring and Autumn Period, but archaeologists have recently found such buckles in tombs of the late Western Zhou in Shandong Province. The buckle was much in vogue from the Warring States Period to the Han Dynasty, when it was widely worn as an ornament of men's dress.

196. Bronze ox   Dress ornament, 5.3 cm long, 3.8 cm wide, Western Han; unearthed in 1956 on the outskirts of Baotou, Inner Mongolia Autonomous Region. As a primary domestic animal for the Huns, the ox played an important role in their economic life. The image of the animal was often seen in their decorative art. The ornament pictured is an exquisite example of the artisanship of the Huns. It depicts a crouching ox and is beautifully shaped.

197. Bronze buckle with figurine of a horseman   Ornament, 5.2 cm long, 3 cm wide, Western Han; unearthed in 1956 at Erlanhugou, Jining, Inner Mongolia Autonomous Region. A great variety of ornamental buckles for the belt were made by the Huns during the Han Dynasty. They reflect, in both shape and decor, the Huns' nomadic life on the grasslands. The buckle pictured here is an example.

198

198. Animal bone with hunting design
Ornament, 7.7 cm high, 4.5 cm in
diameter, Western Han; unearthed in 1954
on the outskirts of Baotou , Inner
Mongolia Autonmous Region. The Huns
lived on livestock farming and hunting
with the bow and arrow. This ornament, a
masterpiece mirroring the Huns' nomadic
life, is covered with designs skillfully
engraved with a needle, depicting flying
birds, running wild boars, and a hunter
with a bow and arrow.

**199. Bronze buckle with openwork
images of two camels** Ornament, 9.6 cm
long, 4.8 cm wide, Western Han;
unearthed in 1983 at Daodunzi, Tongxin,
Ningxia Hui Autonomous Region. This
ornamental buckle was for fastening the
two ends of the leather belt usually worn
by the Huns around the waist. Such
buckles are often decorated with animal
motifs, characteristic of the art of nomadic
tribes on the northern grasslands.

199

200. Pair of bronze goats Carriage ornament, 7.7 cm high, Eastern Han; unearthed in 1967 in Zhangjiakou, Hebei Province. Xiongnu (the Huns) split into two parts, the Northern and Southern Xiongnu, in the early Eastern Han. The Northern Xiongnu controlled the territory north of the Gobi Desert and continued to pose a threat to the Eastern Han. Later, after a devastating attack by the Han army, the Northern Huns who did not surrender fled toward the west and no longer existed as a political entity. The Southern Huns entered the northern borders of the Han empire and became one of its ethnic minorities. The ornament in the picture is a legacy of the Southern Xiongnu. It depicts two standing goats, docile and obedient, with round eyes, long curved horns, and short tails turned upward.

Wuhuan and Xianbei Nationalities

The northeastern part of China was the home of the Wuhuan and Xianbei nationalities and a number of other minorities such as the Fuyu, Woju, Yilou, Gaogouli and Koguryo. Animal husbandry was the main occupation of the Wuhuan and Xianbei, whose cultures were akin to each other. Some of their relics were similar in style to those of the Xiongnu, and they were often found together with Han relics, evidence of the close relations among various nationalities in those days.

201. String of beads   Ornament, Western Han; unearthed in 1956 at Xichagou, Xifeng, Liaoning Province. Large numbers of vitreous beads, round, tubular or resembling the rind of a melon, and pendants, flat and square, rectangular or rhomboid, made of agate, jasper, green or white stone, were found in ancient tombs in Xifeng County, Liaoning Province. These ornaments reflected the unique decorative style of the Donghu people.

202. Bronze horse   Dress ornament, 6.5 cm long , 4.3 cm wide, Western Han; unearthed in 1956 at Xichagou, Xifeng, Liaoning Province. Horses, on which the northern Chinese nomadic people relied for existence, played a great part in their hunting and animal husbandry, and served as a most favorite motif in their decorative art. The bronze crouching horse in the picture is a legacy of the Donghu people.

203

203. Bronze plate with images of mounted warriors Belt ornament, 11.1 cm long, 8.4 cm wide, Western Han; unearthed in 1956 at Xichagou, Xifeng, Liaoning Province. In ancient China the northern nomadic people were generally referred to as the Hu. Xichagou was east of the area where the Huns were active. This bronze artifact, a legacy of the Donghu people, reflects the culture and way of life of nomadic people.

204. Gilded bronze plate with divine-animal motif   Pendant, 11.3 cm long, 7.2 cm wide, Han Dynasty; unearthed in 1980 at Laoheshen, Yushu, Jilin Province. A legacy of the Xianbei people in the Han Dynasty, this pendant features a divine animal with a single curved horn, a raised tail, four feet flying, and wings spread. Looking very much like a flying horse, it by and large conforms to a description in the *Book of the Kingdom of Wei* A divine animal which resembles the horse in appearance and the ox in sound. Since the divine animal design was based on a Xianbei myth, it is of high value in the study of the history and culture of the northeastern ethnic minorities during the Han Dynasty.

205

205. Bronze and iron arrowheads

Weapons, Western Han; unearthed in 1956 at Xichagou, Xifeng, Liaoning Province. These were long-range missiles used by the Donghu people. Retrieved at the same time were arrowheads made of bone and fine-grained stone. Some of them are thin and flat, some have a ridge in the middle, and some are shaped like wings, spearheads or balls with holes. The arrows themselves are mostly made of bamboo. The ball-with-hole arrowheads, made of bronze and functioning like a modern signal pistol, emitted a whistle as they sped swiftly through the air. For this reason they were popularly known as whistling arrowheads.

206. Bronze sleeve

Ornament, 15.6 cm long, 0.3 cm thick, maximum rim 9.2 cm in diameter, minimum rim 5.9 cm in diameter, Han Dynasty; unearthed in 1980 at Laoheshen, Yushu, Jilin Province. This ornament was cast and forged by the Xianbei people with materials from the Central Plains and reflects the level of their handicrafts during the Han Dynasty. It consists of a half sleeve that opens along the middle. It is flat and smooth inside, but has raised circular bands outside. Since such ornaments were found in tombs of women only, they were probably designed specially for Xianbei women in the Han Dynasty.

206

207

Nationalities of the Western Regions

In the early years of the Western Han, there were 36 small states such as Loulan, Ruoqiang, Jingjue, Yutian, Cheshi, Guizi and Shule in the broad areas north and south of the Tianshan Range. Some of them had an agrarian economy, others led a nomadic life. During the reign of Emperor Wu, Zhang Qian was sent as an envoy to the Western Regions to strengthen ties between the Han court and the nationalities in the west. During the reign of Emperor Xuan, the Han court established the Western Regions Administration to exercise jurisdiction over the broad western areas of the country.

208

207. Bronze seal carved "Han Gui Yi Qiang Zhang" 3.5 cm high, 2.3 cm long on each side, Han Dynasty; unearthed in 1953 at Yushigeti, Xayar, Xinjiang Uygur Autonomous Region. The Han Dynasty exercised control over the Qiang people who lived at the northern foot of the Kunlun Mountains, as well as other ethnic minorities in the Western Regions. The seal in the picture, carved with five characters in intaglio in the *zhuan* (seal) style, has a knob in the shape of a crouching sheep. Two of the characters, Gui Yi, was an official title conferred by the Han government on leaders of ethnic minorities in remote areas. It was a seal of the authority vested in the Qiang leader by the Han government.

208. Bronze knife with sheep-head decoration Table knife, 23.3 cm long, 3.9 cm wide, Western Han;collected from Chabuhahe, Xinyuan, Xinjiang Uygur Autonomous Region. This was a typical article of the ancient Wusun nationality, who were active in the Yili River valley after moving westward in the early Western Han. The Wusun people, who boasted fine horses, led a nomadic life, wandering from place to place in search of pastureland for their flocks or herds. In the tombs of the Wusun people were often found sheep bones and small iron daggers, some daggers stuck in the bone, an indication that they lived on a diet of meat and butter milk.

209-1

209. Felt hat and cowhide boots

Articles for preparing the body for burial, Western Han; unearthed in 1934 in the Loulan ruins, Lop Nur, Xinjiang Uygur Autonomous Region. Loulan, a famous city along the Silk Road, was built in the late Western Han or early Eastern Han. The early tombs of Loulan, in which the dead persons were placed in peculiar coffins shaped like boats, are scattered along the banks of the Konqi River north of Lop Nur. Because of the arid climate, well-preserved mummies, wearing white weasel felt hats decorated with feathers, woollen cloaks, cowhide boots, and strings of stone, clamshell or jade beads at the waist or wrist, were found in some of the Loulan tombs.

209-2

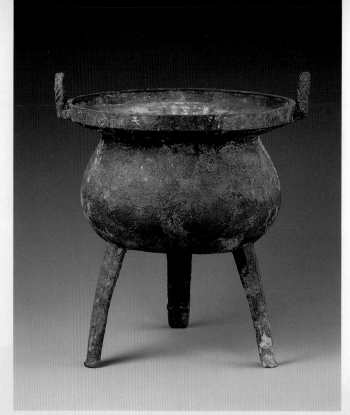

210

Baiyue Nationality

Different branches of the Baiyue nationality lived along the southeastern coast and in areas in the south. Those in present-day Zhejiang and Fujian provinces were called Eastern Ou and Minyue, and those in Guangdong and Guangxi were called Southern Yue, Luoyue and Western Ou. Relics unearthed from these areas possess the characteristics of Yue culture, but also include features of Han culture, a result of the merging of the two cultures.

211

210. Yue-style bronze *ding* Cooking vessel, 28.5 cm high, rim 30 cm in diameter, Western Han; unearthed in 1983 from the King of Southern Yue's tomb at Xianggangshan, Guangzhou, Guangdong Province. The Yue-style *ding*, a typical bronze pot of the Southern Yue that first appeared in pre-Qin days, features legs that point outward. *Ding* vessels made in this style in the Han Dynasty are generally crude, unadorned, and covered with a thick layer of soot, indicating that they were for practical use.

211.Bronze jar with a chain loop Wine vessel, 30.5 cm high, rim 11.5 cm in diameter at the top and 17.7 at the bottom, Western Han; unearthed in 1955 in Gui

213

212

County, Guangxi Zhuang Autonomous Region. The Yue nationality, known as "a hundred Yue" because of its numerous branches, lived in south China during the Warring States Period and the Qin and Han dynasties. The First Emperor of Qin, after unifying the country, established prefectures and counties in the Yue areas. Emperor Wu of Han expanded the territory to nine prefectures, where the economy developed with the introduction of advanced tools and techniques of production from the Central Plains. The bronze jar in the picture has the features of both Yue and Han vessels, reflecting the gradual merging of the Han and Yue people as they lived together in the Qin-Han period.

212. Pottery *pao* flask Wine vessel, 27.2 cm high, rim 2 cm in diameter at the top and 12.5 at the

bottom, Western Han; unearthed in 1953 at Longshenggang, Guangzhou, Guangdong Province. This flask is so named because it was modeled on a gourd called *pao* in Chinese. Flasks of this kind were retrieved from tombs of the early Eastern Han and especially the mid Western Han in the Guangzhou area, and have distinct local characteristics. They were later replaced by pottery bottles.

213. Three-legged earthen pot Container, 9 cm high, belly 15.3 in diameter, Western Han; unearthed in 1957 at Overseas Chinese New Village in Guangzhou, Guangdong Province. Three-legged pots, small, uniquely shaped, occasionally with carbonized particles or powder inside, were found in all types of tombs of early Western Han in the Guangzhou area. Retrieved from the tombs were also three-legged boxes and jointed jars, all with distinct local features.

214. Four jointed earthen jars Container for dry fruits or condiments, 17.5 cm long, 10.1 cm high, Westerm Han; unearthed in 1957 at Overseas Chinese New Village in Guangzhou, Guangdong Province. Two, three, four and five jointed earthen jars, uniquely shaped and rich in local color, were in vogue in what is now Guangdong Province during the early Western Han Dynasty. By the Eastern Han they had become obsolete.

214

215. Rabbit-shaped bronze water dropper

Writing article, 5 cm high, 15 cm long,
Western Han; unearthed in 1957 in Wuzhou,
Guangxi Zhuang Autonomous Region. This
vessel was for dripping water onto inkstone to
prepare ink. Most ancient devices of this sort
were shaped like animals that had some
connection with water. The rabbit symbolizes
the moon, which, according to ancient Chinese
philosophy, is feminine and related to water.

216. Bronze drum with *wuzhu*-coin motif   90

cm in diameter, 57.2 cm high, weight 75.4 kg,
Han Dynasty; unearthed in 1954 in Cenxi,
Guangxi Zhuang Autonomous Region. In
ancient times the bronze drum was a weighty
object symbolizing wealth and power to the
ethnic minorities in south and southwest
China. It could be used as a war drum, a
musical instrument in ceremonies, or storage
for the bones of the dead. The drum in the
picture is decorated with a *wuzhu-coin* motif
on the top surface and all over the body,
suggesting close ties between the economies
and cultures of the Han and the minority
nationalities in southwest China.

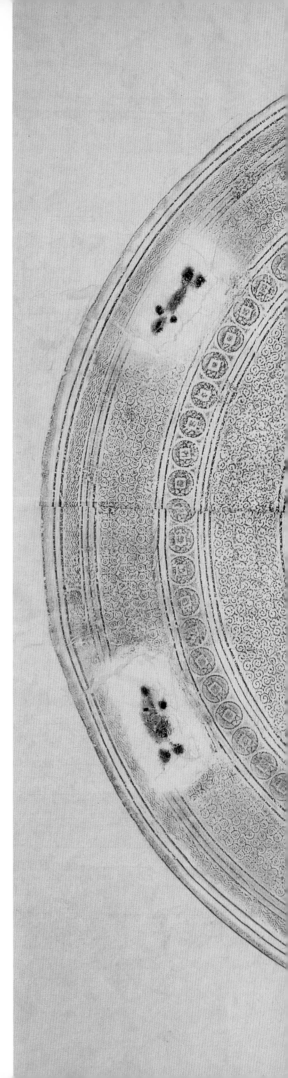

215

Southwestern Yi

The nationalities Yelang, Dian, Qiongdu, Xi, Kunming, Zuodu, Ranmang and Baima inhabiting modern Yunnan, Guizhou and the western part of Sichuan were collectively known as the Southwestern Yi in the Han Dynasty. Among them the Dian people had reached an advanced stage of bronze culture at the time. Most of their bronzeware had decorative designs portraying social phenomena in their day. In the Han Dynasty prefectures were set up in the southwestern areas, strengthening relations between the Han and the minority nationalities there.

217

217. Tiger-shaped bronze buckle
13.3 cm long, 5.5 cm wide, Western Han; unearthed in Zigui, Hubei Province. The tiger was an animal worshipped by the ancient Ba people. A nationality good at fishing and hunting, the Ba originally inhabited the Qing River valley and were active in the Three Gorges area during the Shang and Zhou dynasties. Their descendants, known as Bandunman or Binren, still lived there in the Han Dynasty. The buckle in the picture is a legacy of the Ba nationality.

218. Bronze *chunyu* Percussion instrument, 59 cm high, Western Han; allegedly discovered in Chengdu, Sichuan Province. The area in what is now Sichuan Province had a highly developed economy and culture during the Qin-Han period. The Bashu culture, well known in Chinese history, originated and developed there. Though in the ensuing periods it gradually merged into the Han culture, the national culture of China, traces of the once splendid Bashu culture can still be found in Sichuan. The *chunyu* in the picture, with a tiger-shaped knob, bulging shoulders, and an elliptic cylindrical body, is a legacy of the Ba or Shu people in the period from the Warring States to the early Western Han. It furnishes valuable material for studying the ancient Bashu culture.

219-1

219. King of Dian's seal   1.8 cm high, side 2.3 cm long, weight 89.5 g, Western Han; unearthed in 1956 from the King of Dian's tomb at Shizhaishan, Jinning, Yunnan Province. The seal, carved with four characters ("meaning" King of Dian's seal) in intaglio in the *zhuan* (seal)script, is made of gold with a snake-shaped knob. Jinning County belonged to Yizhou Prefecture in the Han Dynasty. According to *Records of the Historian*, Emperor Wu of Han set up Yizhou Prefecture in the Kingdom of Dian in 109 BC, the second year of the Yuanfeng reign, and conferred on the King of Dian a seal of authority to continue his rule over the Dian people. The seal verifies the account in the book. It must be a copy, however, for the original would have been handed down from generation to generation and could not have been used as a burial object. The imitation was crudely made, and the carved characters do not strictly conform to the seal script.

220. Bronze cowrie container with tiger-shaped ears and statuettes of seven buffaloes   43.5 cm high, 21.8 cm in diameter at the bottom, Western Han; unearthed at Shizhaishan, Jinning, Yunnan Province. A cylindrical vessel larger at the top than at the bottom, it has two symmetric tiger-shaped ears on the sides of a contracted waist and statuettes of seven buffaloes on its lid. Bronzes with the buffalo motif are the most numerous items among the archaeological finds at Shizhaishan, indicating that animal husbandry still held a very important place in the essentially agricultural society of the Dian people. Possession of buffaloes was one of the criteria by which wealth was measured at the time. Inclusion of vessels featuring the buffalo in a tomb would show the wealth of the tomb occupant.

219-2

221. Bronze cowrie container with a scene of sacrificial ceremony 53 cm high, lid 32 cm in diameter, late Western Han; unearthed at Shizhaishan, Jinning, Yunnan Province. Over 300 cowries were found in the container when it was unearthed. Cast on the lid was a sculpture in the round, depicting a pile-supported building where 127 persons (not including damaged figurines) attended a sacrificial ceremony held by the King of Dian. Ancient books record that whenever a major event occurred the Dian people would hold a grand ceremony with many offerings on a sacrificial altar. The sculpture in the picture vividly portrays such a scene.

221-1

221-2

222. Circular bronze ornament with sculpted monkeys along its edge
Pendant, 12.3 cm in diameter, Western Han; unearthed at Shizhaishan, Jinning, Yunnan Province. Archaeologists believe that this circular ornament, trimmed with the images of 20 interlocked monkeys, originally had a button made of precious stone in the middle and was surrounded with tiny pieces of turquoise. Hanging from the waist belt, it served as a protective talisman.

223-1

223. Bronze cowrie container with a weaving scene   21 cm high, Western Han; unearthed at Shizhaishan, Jinning, Yunnan Province. This vessel features bronze statuettes of 18 female family slaves cast on a lid less than 25 cm in diameter. Sitting with their legs stretched out, the slaves are shown spinning and weaving for their owner in an open-air workshop. The vessel provides important material for studying the weaving craft of the Dian people in the Han Dynasty.

223-2

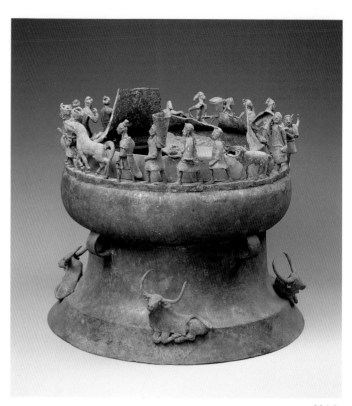

224-1

224. Bronze cowrie container with a scene of paying tribute   Remaining part 39.5 cm high, mid Western Han; unearthed at Shizhaishan, Jinning, Yunnan Province. The original container, according to archaeologists, consisted of two drumlike parts; the upper part had been damaged when it was unearthed. Cast along the border of the remaining part were 21 three-dimensional statuettes of men, horses and buffaloes. The men can be divided into seven groups according to their dress, hairstyle and manner of proceeding, each group consisting of two to four people and representing a tribe. The man at the head of each group, richly dressed and wearing a sword, is presumably the tribal chief, who is followed by his tribe members carrying goods or leading horses or buffaloes. Viewed as a whole, it must be a scene representing the paying of tribute to the King of Dian by tribes that acknowledge allegiance to him.

224-2

224-3 ▷

225

225. Bronze ornament depicting a tiger with a deer on its back   Pendant, 13 cm long, 10.5 cm wide, Western Han; unearthed at Shizhaishan, Jinning, Yunnan Province. This ornamental clasp vividly portrays a fierce tiger walking with a wounded deer on its back. A meek animal, the deer was often shown to be chased or devoured by fierce animals in Dian bronzes.

226

226. Bronze clasp depicting a buffalo fighting a tiger Pendant, 17 cm long, 8.5 cm wide, Western Han; unearthed at Shizhaishan, Jinning, Yunan Province. This ornament successfully catches a life-and-death struggle between a buffalo and a tiger.

227. Bronze spearhead with hanging figurines Weapon, 38 cm long, Western Han; unearthed in 1956—57 at Shizhaishan, Jinning, Yunan Province. Over a thousand bronze weapons, including *zhuo*, *cha*, spears, dagger-axes, swords, axes, battle-axes and cross-bows, were retrieved in the 1950's from tombs of the Dian people at Shizhaishan. Some are real weapons used by the tomb occupants during their lifetime, while others are articles to be carried by guards of honor. They display the high level of Dian bronze technology. The spearhead pictured here features figurines of two naked captives, with their hair worn in topknots and their hands tied behind their backs, hanging from two thin chains fastened to the two sides of the blade. Rich in local color and with a novel shape, it is a priceless example of the Dian people's bronze weapons.

228. Gilded bronze ornament with figures of four dancers Pendant, 11.7 cm high, 15 cm long, Western Han; unearthed at Shizhaishan, Jinning, Yunnan Province. The four figurines in the picture, wearing identical costume and hairdress, represent dancers of an ethnic minority in southwest China. Since ancient times the ethnic minorities in that part of China have been known for their singing and dancing, usually accompanied with the *sheng* (reed pipe) and drums.

229-2

230. Bronze ornament with men-and-buffalo motif   Pendant, 4 cm high, 6.5 cm wide, late Warring States to early Western Han; unearthed at Lijiashan, Jiangchuan, Yunnan Province. This ornament features a standing buffalo and three barefoot men wearing jackets with buttons down the front, tightly fastened belts,and earrings, their hair in topknots. One of the men is roping the buffalo while the other two hold its tail. Judging from the other relics unearthed at Shizhaishan and Lijiashan, the three men must be of the Dian nationality.

229. The bronze *zhuo*   Weapon, 26.1 cm long, 14.8 cm high, late Warring States to early Western Han; unearthed at Lijiashan, Jiangchuan, Yunnan Province. Bronze *zhuo* was a common weapon of the Dian nationality in the Han Dynasty.

230

231-2

231. Bronze pillow 70 cm long, 13 cm wide, 36.4 cm high, Western Han; unearthed at Lijiashan, Jiangchuan, Yunnan Province. Shaped like a saddle, this bronze pillow has a three-dimensional sculpture of a standing buffalo on each of the two ends that turn upward and relief sculptures of three standing buffaloes in the middle. In both ancient and modern times the buffalo was a symbol of wealth to many ethnic minorities in southwest China. That is why people in that area often hang a buffalo head on the roof ridge or in front of the door. The buffaloes featured on the bronze pillow might also be a symbol of wealth.

◁ 231-1

Science and Culture of the Han Dynasty

During the two-Han period brilliant achievements were made in paper making, astronomy, mathematics, seismology, medical science, sports and physical fitness, as well as in philosophy, history, literature and art.

Invention of Paper

Paper making was one of the four great inventions of ancient China and a major contribution to world culture. During the Western Han the Chinese people, perceiving that floating catkins could coagulate to form thin sheets, made rough plant fiber paper from waste linen. In the Eastern Han, Cai Lun, improving on existing techniques and widening the source of raw materials, made a finer grade of plant fiber paper which people called "Marquis Cai's paper." Because it was inexpensive, could be mass produced, and was easy to write on, such paper gradually replaced silk fabrics and bamboo slips as the most important writing material. Later, the technique of paper making was introduced to many parts of the world, resulting in an epoch-making revolution in humanity's writing materials.

232

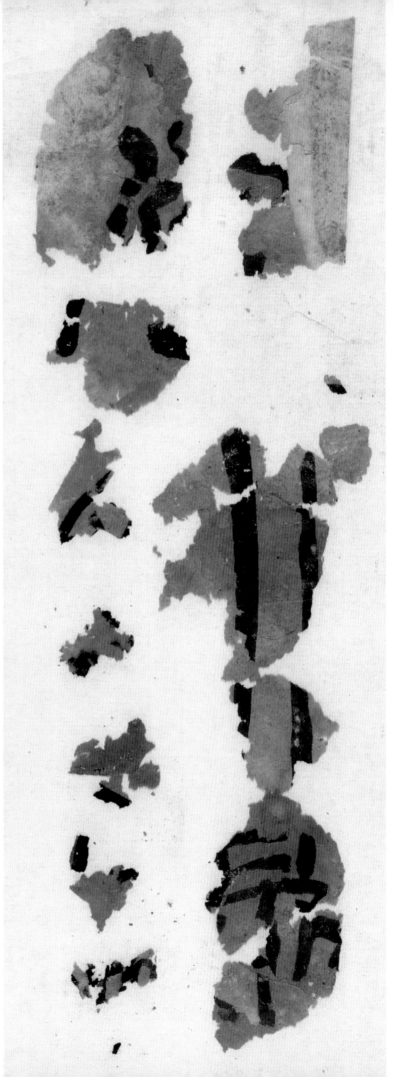

232. Fufeng paper   Remaining part 7.4 cm long, 6.8 cm wide, Western Han; unearthed in 1978 in Fufeng, Shaanxi Province. With hemp as raw material, Fufeng paper is milky yellow and contains many fibrous bundles and rope ends not yet entirely unraveled. It has a coarse, loose texture and unevenly distributed fibers, but is tough and easy to fold. As a primitive form of paper, it is unfit for writing on.

233. Hantanpo paper with written characters   Eastern Han, unearthed in 1974 at Hantanpo, Wuwei, Gansu Province. Made of hemp, Hantanpo paper has a fine, close texture, a smooth surface with fibers evenly distributed, and few fibrous bundles. The pieces of Hantanpo paper in the picture, made in Eastern Han, bear several characters in *lishu* (official script); two of them can be recognized as "qing bei." Writing paper of the Eastern Han was also found in the Xinjiang Uygur Autonomous Region, in Dunhuang City of Gansu Province, and on the banks of the Ejina River in the Inner Mongolia Autonomous Region. Discovery of the earliest plant-fiber writing paper confirms that the improvements made by Cai Lun, a second-century court official, in the material and technique of paper making did raise the quality of paper and production efficiency, paving the way for replacing silk and bamboo slips with paper as China's principal writing material.

234. Inkslab and rub stone   Inkslab 9.5
cm in diameter and 1.5 to 1.6 cm thick,
with a 3.5 cm-high rub stone, Western
Han; unearthed in 1975 at
Fenghuangshan, Jiangling, Hubei Province.
Inkslabs are a time-honored Chinese
handicraft article and an important
writing tool. The earliest inkslab
discovered dates back to the late Warring
States Period. Many Han inkslabs, made of
stone or clay or coated with lacquer, are
still extant. They were either handed
down from the Han Dynasty or unearthed
from Han sites. An inkslab complete with a
rub stone suggests that during the
Western Han Dynasty it was not yet
possible to produce ink sticks with
adequate hardness.

235

236

235. Inkslab in a lacquer case 21.5 cm long, 7.4 cm wide, Western Han; unearthed in 1978 at Jinqueshan, Linyi, Shandong Province. The inkslab, in a case lacquered in reddish brown both inside and outside, was made of slate. Inside the case was a square rub stone, 0.2 cm thick and 2.5 cm long on each side, glued to a square board 1.1 cm thick and 2.5 cm long on each side. The user held the board while pressing the rub stone against the inkslab. Prior to the advent of ink sticks, ink was prepared by placing a tiny ink ball on the inkslab and adding a little water before rubbing it against the inkslab with the rub stone.

236. Ink stick shaped like a pinecone
Writing tool, 6.2 cm high, 3 cm in diameter, Eastern Han; unearthed in 1974 on the outskirts of Guyuan County, Ningxia Hui Autonomous Region. Ink was first made in China by pressing ink powders against an inkslab with a rub stone. Ink pellets were used instead of ink powders in the early Western Han at the latest. Still later, ink was made into sticks that could be held and rubbed directly on an inkslab. The ink stick in the picture is light and solid, and the ink made by rubbing it with water on an inkslab is pure, clear and as black and sticky as lacquer. Though it had been buried underground for over 1,800 years, it was as good as fresh from the mold, without even a minute crack, when it was unearthed. During the Han Dynasty, Yumi (present-day Qianyang, Shaanxi Province) was famous for its ink sticks. The pinecone-shaped ink stick, unearthed at a place not far from Yumi, may have been produced there.

237-1

Astronomy and Mathematics

During the two-Han period, important discoveries and inventions were made in astronomy, mathematics and seismology. In the *History of the Han Dynasty*: *Astronomy*, it is recorded that in the sixth month of the first year (134 BC) of Yuanguang of Emperor Wu's reign, a nova was seen at Fang. It was the earliest record of a nova. Since then, down to the end of the 17th century, about 70 novae have been recorded in ancient Chinese books. The earliest recording of sun spots was made in China in the first year (28 BC) of Western Han emperor Cheng's reign titled Heping. By the end of the Ming Dynasty, more than 100 recordings of sun spots were made in Chinese history books, providing abundant data for the study of the sunspot cycle. *Nine Chapters of Mathematical Arts* is a mathematic work of the Eastern Han that summarized the development of Chinese mathematics from Zhou and Qin to the Han Dynasty. The book introduced many new concepts that were the most advanced in the world at that time, such as the operations of positive and negative numbers, the proportional algorithm, the four basic operations of fractions, how to extract square and cube roots, methods of solving quadratic equations with one unknown quantity and simultaneous linear equations.

In the first year (AD 132) of the reign titled Yangjia of the Eastern Han, Zhang Heng invented a seismograph in Luoyang, the first instrument of its kind in the world.

237. Sundial   Time-measuring instrument, 27.4 cm long on each side, 3.5 cm thick, Han Dynasty; unearthed in 1897 at Togtoh, Inner Mongolia Autonomous Region. Made of compact argillaceous marble in the Han Dynasty, this is the earliest Chinese sundial extant, providing important material for studying the development of China's time-measuring instruments. It consisted of a square dial

and two gnomons, known as *zhengbiao* and *youyi*; the gnomons have been lost. The sundial was often used in the Han Dynasty to remedy the defect of the clepsydra, which was inaccurate owing to the uneven speed of the flow of water.

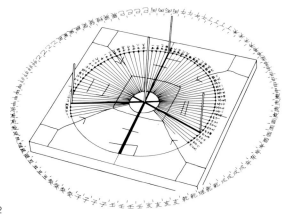

237-2

237-3 ▷

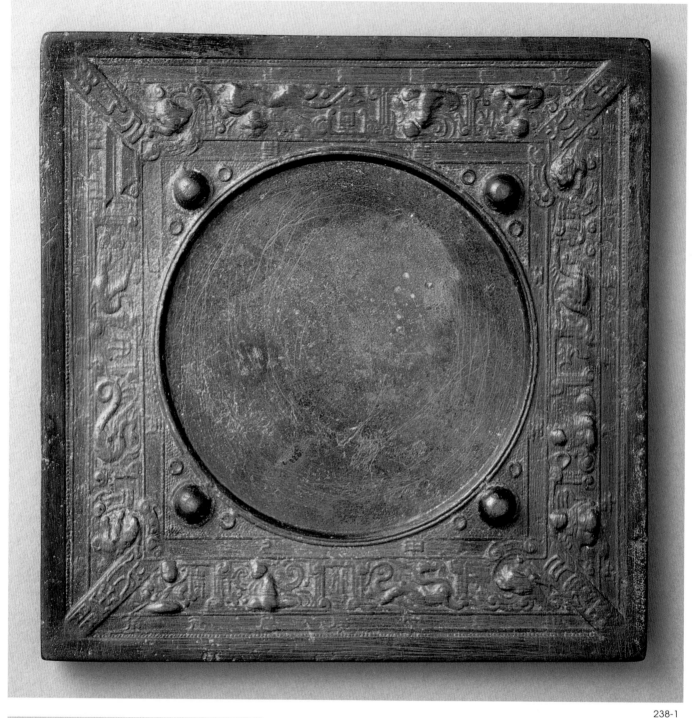

238-1

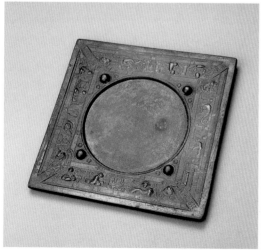

238-2

238. Bronze "Earthly Plate"

Divination article, 0.6 cm thick, 14.3 cm long on each side, Eastern Han. The divination instrument consisted of a circular and a square plate, symbolizing heaven and earth respectively. The circular Heavenly Plate has been lost. The instrument was designed according to the ancient Chinese notion that heaven was round and earth square. There were many types of divination. The square Earthly Plate in the picture is of the *liuren* type. Marked on the Heavenly Plate of the *liuren* type was the Big Dipper surrounded by the twenty-eight Chinese zodiacal constellations and twelve gods. On the Earthly Plate were the Heavenly Stems and Earthly Branches, the four gates for heaven, earth, men and ghosts, and luminous bodies corresponding to the twenty-eight zodiacal constellations. Divination was done by turning the Heavenly Plate leftward and interpreting the positions on the Earthly Plate that corresponded to the Dipper's handle and the twelve gods.

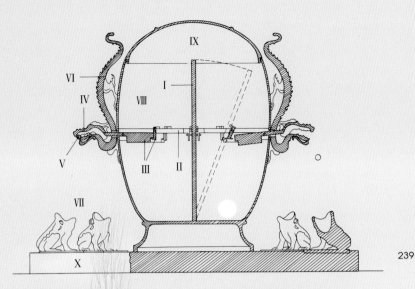

239

Key to numerals: I. *duzhu* **II.** *badao* **III.** trigger **IV.** dragon head
V. bronze ball **VI.** dragon body **VII.** bronze toad **VIII.**body of
seismograph **IX.** lid of seismograph **X.** stand

**239. Reconstructed Seismograph
(sectional drawing)** This is the world's
first seismograph, invented by Zhang
Heng, a multi-talented Chinese scientist of
the Eastern Han, in 132, the first year of
Emperor Shundi's Yangjia reign, in
Luoyang. Cast in fine bronze, it was about
1.94 meters in diameter and shaped like a
wine jar with a lid. The main part of the
mechanism is a *duzhu*, a pendulumlike
rod, surrounded by eight groups of lever
mechanisms, known as *badao*, distributed
in eight directions and connected to the
body of the seismograph. Eight bronze
dragons are fixed in corresponding
positions on the outside of the
seismograph. Each dragon has a small
bronze ball in its mouth, beneath which a
bronze toad opens its mouth upward.

When an earthquake occurs, the seismic
waves are transmitted to the seismograph
and the *duzhu* inclines in the direction of
the quake, triggering the lever in the head
of the dragon there. The dragon opens its
mouth and releases the ball, which falls
into the mouth of the toad with a clang.
The monitoring personnel thus know the
time of the quake and the direction in
which it occurs. Zhang Heng's
seismograph, which could detect even a
mild tremor that men did not feel, was
developed over 1,700 years earlier than a
similar device in Europe. It was a
remarkable achievement of ancient
Chinese science and technology.

240. Lead rods Calculating objects, 5-16
cm long, Western Han; unearthed in 1982
on the outskirts of Xi'an, Shaanxi Province.
Rods were widely used as calculating
objects before the invention of the abacus.
Laid crosswise or lengthwise, they could
be used to express any given number and
to calculate by the decimal system. They
were very popular during the Spring and
Autumn and Warring States Periods, and
were made of bamboo, lead or bone in the
Han Dynasty. The rods pictured here are
in the form of long, narrow and flat strips
of even thickness, indicating that
calculation by rods had evolved to
perfection by the Han Dynasty.

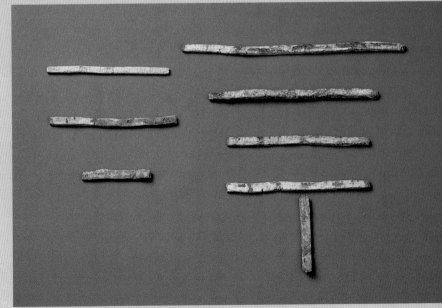

240

Medical and Pharmaceutical Science

A basic system of Chinese traditional medicine was set up in the Han Dynasty, and important achievements were made in pathological studies, treatment of diseases, the use of medicinal herbs, acupuncture and moxibustion, and sports as a way of keeping fit. Zhang Zhongjing laid the foundation of dialectical treatment in Chinese traditional medicine. Hua Tuo, another medical talent, was the first surgeon in the world to use general drug anaesthesia in major operations.

241. Gold acupuncture needle Medical instrument, Western Han; unearthed in 1968 from the Liu Sheng tomb in Mancheng, Hebei Province. Four gold acupuncture needles, 6.5-7 cm long and 0.12-0.18 cm in diameter, were retrieved from the Western Han tomb of Liu Sheng, Prince Jing of Zhongshan. The needles, thicker than modern ones, are round in the lower part and angular, with a hole, in the upper part. Two of them are of the filiform type, one has a three-edged tip used in venous pricking, and the fourth, a blunt needle, was used in *dianci* treatment. The needle in the picture is of the filiform type. Acupuncture and moxibustion are two unique therapeutic methods developed by the ancient Chinese. Discovery of the gold needles furnishes valuable material for studying those ancient methods.

241

242. Rubbing of a stone engraving showing acupuncture treatment (detail) Decorative engraving in a tomb chamber, 94.5 cm long, 91.5 cm wide, 24 cm thick, Eastern Han; unearthed in Weishan, Shandong Province. The stone engraving consists of three parts. The middle part depicts a creature with a human face and a bird body, who is holding a needle ready to apply acupuncture to a group of people. The creature probably represents Bian Que, a famous doctor in the Warring States Period, for his name literally means a magpie, a bird symbolizing good luck in ancient China.

242

243. Bronze basin Medical vessel, rim 27.6 cm in diameter, 8.3 cm high, Western Han; unearthed in 1968 from the Liu Sheng tomb in Mancheng, Hebei Province. Two characters, *yi gong*, meaning medical workers, were engraved on the rim of the basin. In the Han Dynasty the official in charge of medical matters in a vassal state was called Yi Gong Zhang. The basin has two riveted joints, one on the rim and the other on the bottom, indicating that it has been repaired. A vessel of the family of Liu Sheng, Prince of Zhongshan, it is the earliest medical basin discovered.

243-2

243-1

Literature, History, Philosophy and Religion

During the reign of Emperor Wu of the Han Dynasty, Confucianism became predominant and the Confucian classics were made the official philosophy, but Wang Chong (AD 27– c.100), an ideologist of Eastern Han, expounded and espoused materialist ideology. Han dynasty folk songs represented by "The Ailing Wife", "Orphans", "The Hoary-headed Man", and "The Roadside Mulberry" were full of vitality; poems with five characters to a line began to appear; and prose and Han *fu* (rhyme prose) were composed in great numbers. Many celebrated men of letters, among them Jia Yi, Sima Xiangru and Zhang Heng, emerged and notable works like *Records of the Historian* by Sima Qian and *History of the Han Dynasty* by Ban Gu appeared one after another. In religion, Taoism began to flourish and exotic Buddhism was introduced into China.

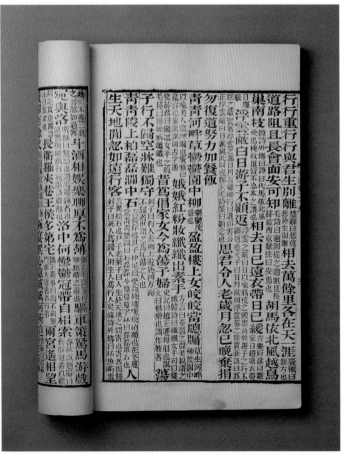

244

244. *Nineteen Old Poems* (a Qing Dynasty reprint published in the eighth year of the Tongzhi reign) Anonymous poems of the Han Dynasty. The 19 poems in this book, all in the form of five-character lines, were selected by Xiao Tong, a crown prince of the Liang of Southern Dynasties, from the Han Dynasty lyric verses written by men of letters under the influence of folk songs. Most of the poems express strong personal feelings such as the sadness of lovers' partings, the sorrow and woe in a girl's heart, the longing for parents of a wandering son, and the resentment of young people at having passed their years in vain. They reflect people's dissatisfaction with the political turmoil of the time — the root cause of social instability and the breaking up of families. Inheriting the fine traditions of the *Book of Songs* and the *Verse of Chu* while assimilating ideas from folk songs, *Nineteen Old Poems* displays the remarkable achievements in poetry and exerted a profound influence on the poetic works of later periods.

245. Fragment of tablet of "Xiping Stone Classics" 45 cm high, Eastern Han. "Xiping Stone Classics," the earliest Confucian classics engraved on stone by government order,originally stood in the Imperial College of the Han Dynasty on the outskirts of Luoyang (present-day Yanshi, Henan Province). In 175, the fourth year of the Xiping reign of the Eastern Han emperor Lingdi, Cai Yong and other scholars made hand-written copies in *lishu* (official script) of seven Confucian classics, the *Book of Songs, Book of History, Book of Changes, Book of Rites, Spring and Autumn Annals, Spring and Autumn Annals with Commentary by Gongyang Gao and the Analects of Confucius*. It took nine years to have these copies engraved on 46 stone tablets, which became standard versions of the seven classics. It was a heroic undertaking towards popularizing Confucianism. According to history books, an incessant stream of horses and carriages carried visitors to where the stone classics stood, causing traffic jams. No complete stone tablet survived the chaos brought about by war at the end of the Han Dynasty. Fragments of the tablets, however,have been unearthed from time to time, since the Song Dynasty.

宇　車　子　臨　實　員　乾
聞　滑　言　庠　滅　項　博　壐
留　心　吏　以　孝　覆　舒　紅　若　家　沫
雜　楷　古　人　事　斛　相　陰
與　先　棟　重　版　文　覺
觀　校　正　競　文
官　庠　序
中　郎　將
論
顛
下
大

246. *Records of the Historian*   Written by
Sima Qian, historian of the Western Han.
Records of the Historian is the first
systematized and comprehensive history of
China. Divided into Basic Annals, Tables,
Treatises, Hereditary Houses and Lives, it
contains 130 sections in all, and more than
half a million words. A monumental work of
high historical value,it records some 3,000
years of history, from the reign of the
legendary Yellow Emperor down to that of
Emperor Wu of Han. The method of
presenting history through character
sketches, which Sima Qian created, became
the accepted way of recording official
history. *Records of the Historian* is also fine
literature. Using a rich vocabulary, it gives
vivid accounts of historical figures and
events, exerting a profound influence on
both Chinese history and literature.

246

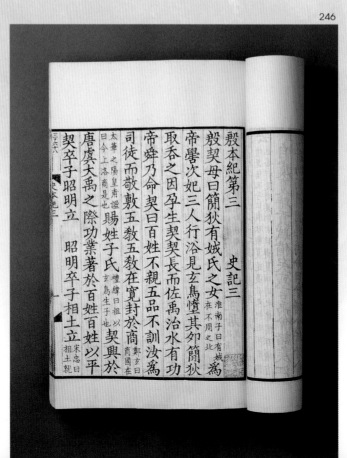

247

247. Pottery jar with writing in vermilion

Funerary object, 23 cm high, Eastern Han; unearthed in 1957 at Sanlicun, Chang'an, Shaanxi Province. Taoism, a religion indigenous to China, traced its origin to ancient sorcery and divination. It was in the embryonic stage in the late Western Han, and had an increasing number of followers in the Yellow River valley and the middle and lower reaches of the Yangtze River by the late Eastern Han. Honoring Laozi as the founder of their religion, the Taoists practiced sorcery and the use of figures and incantations. The jar in the picture bears characters in *lishu* (official script) written by a Taoist in vermilion, which was some sort of blessing on the dead. The item reflects the widespread influence of Taoism in the late Eastern Han.

248. Fragment of stone railing with inscriptions in Kharosthi

Eastern Han; collected in 1924 from Luoyang, Henan Province. Buddhism originated in ancient India. Its founder, Siddhartha Gautama, was popularly known by his title Sakyamuni, meaning the sage of the Sakya family. The goal of Buddhist discipline is escape from all forms of suffering and the eventual attainment of Buddhahood. Buddhism was first introduced into China in the late Western Han. In the Eastern Han Buddhist scriptures were translated into Chinese and Buddhist temples built; it gradually became an influential religion in China. The fragment in the picture is of the railings around a stone well that bear inscriptions in Kharosthi (a language of ancient India) recording the activities of Buddhist monks and priests. It is a legacy of the Dayuezhi people who lived in Luoyang during the reign of Emperor Lingdi (AD 168—189) of Eastern Han.

248

249

Arts

Painting and sculpture were highly developed in the Western Han. Paintings included frescoes, woodcuts, and paintings on silk, lacquerware and vessels. Sculpture included pottery, stone and wood carvings and bronze work. They were rich and varied in form and very realistic in style. Their themes were mostly reflections of the unprecedented wealth and power of the Han empire. Music, dancing and acrobatics became richer and more colorful through assimilating foreign elements. The most popular kinds were acrobatic wrestling, the long-sleeve dance, turban dance, seven-plate dance, drum dance, dance accompanied by big drums, as well as ethnic music and dances introduced from the Western Regions.

249. Pottery crane Funerary object, 67 cm high, Eastern Han; unearthed in the Dongshan Irrigated Area, Chengdu, Sichuan Province. In ancient Chinese legends the crane was a mount for immortals, a symbol of longevity. The crane in the picture, standing erect and holding its head high, seems about to take off with a cry. Succinct in style, it is a masterpiece of Han Dynasty sculpture.

250. Man riding a horse (stone sculpture) Funerary object, 78 cm high, 77.2 cm long, Eastern Han; unearthed in 1955 in Wangdu, Hebei Province. Sculpture of Eastern Han is quite different from that of Western Han in style. While the latter stresses succinctness, showing only a rough outline of the object, the former uses lines to delineate details such as the dress of human beings and the feathers of fowls. The painted stone sculpture in the picture, made from a single piece of limestone, is vivid and lifelike in detail. However, it is crude, primitive and vigorous when viewed as a whole. The man on the horse, apparently a servant, wears black headgear, a red

jacket with a white cloud pattern, and a pair of pink broad-legged trousers with a red cloud pattern. Holding an oval wine vessel in his left hand and two fish in his right, he looks pleased with the things he has bought. A sculpture with such a theme was rare in the Han Dynasty. It is a gem of Han stone sculpture.

250-1

250-2 ▷

251-2

251. Storytelling to the accompaniment of a drum (clay figurine)　Funerary object, 56 cm high, Eastern Han; unearthed in 1957 at Tianhuishan, Chengdu, Sichuan Province. Storytelling as a genre of entertainment was very popular in the Han Dynasty. The sculpture in the picture, rich in local color, portrays a barechested, barefooted storyteller. Holding a drum under his left arm and a stick in his right hand, he tells stories in a humorous, dramatizing manner. The discovery of many similar figurines in Eastern Han tombs in Sichuan Province indicates the popularity of storytelling in the ancient Shu territory.

252. Painted clay figurine of a dancer
Funerary object, 50 cm high, Western Han; unearthed in 1954 at Baijiakou, Xi'an, Shaanxi Province. With unification of the country, social stability and economic prosperity, the Western Han Dynasty witnessed a flourishing scene of music and dancing, arts much in favor with its nobles and officials. The long-sleeve dance, free, easy and graceful, was one of the dance popular at the time. The dancers wave their long sleeves in the air, creating a fascinating scene of flying rainbows. The figurine in the picture, a gem of Han sculpture, captures the beauty of a long-sleeve dancer with her lithe and graceful movements.

253. Wooden monkey Funerary object, 11.5 cm high, Eastern Han;unearthed in 1957 at Mozuizi, Wuwei, Gansu Province. Painted in red and black , this wooden sculpture portrays a kneeling monkey with its head slightly lowered, its left arm resting on the ground, and its right arm bent upward to the mouth as if tasting some food. Succinct in style, it is an excellent small carving of the Han Dynasty, quite like a modern one.

254-2

254. Pottery stage Funerary object, 99 cm high, Eastern Han; unearthed in 1975 at Dawangdian, Guoyang, Anhui Province. A four-storied structure, this pottery replica of a stage is made of laterite paste coated with green glaze. The top floor is a drum tower. The stage, with three sides enclosed and one side open, is on the second floor. It has a backstage, an entrance and an exit. On the stage are figurines of five performers. Discovery of the pottery replica puts forward the date of the stage's initial appearance in China from the Northern Song Dynasty (10th century) to the late Eastern Han (3rd century), and repudiates the view that the traditional Chinese stage was open on three sides and that the stage with three sides enclosed and only one side open was introduced from the West. The pottery stage is, therefore, of great value in Chinese and even world theatrical history.

254-1

255-1

255. Brick engraving of horses, carriages and acrobats

Decorative engraving in a tomb chamber, 105.5 cm long, 35.6 cm wide, 6.7 cm thick, Han Dynasty. The right half of the engraving shows a procession of horses and carriages. On the left half is an astounding acrobatic feat popular during the Han Dynasty. The acrobatic feat requires much strength, skill and courage. A long pole, at the top of which sits a man, is fixed in a carriage. The man holds one end of a rope, with the other end tied to the top of a long pole fixed in a carriage behind him. As the two carriages move, a second man climbs the pole fixed in the second carriage, while a third man performs a handstand in the middle of the rope.

255-2

256. Watching acrobatics (brick engraving) Decorative engraving in a tomb chamber, 40 cm long on each side, Eastern Han; unearthed in 1954 at Yangzishan, Chengdu, Sichuan Province. In the Han Dynasty it was customary to entertain guests at a feast with music, dancing and a variety show. The performance took place as the host and guests sat on the ground to one side. The brick engraving in the picture depicts just such a scene: a man and a woman, sitting on the ground, watch with interest performances of the towel dance and juggling with balls and bottles to the accompaniment of drums and panpipes. With its vivid images and rich flavor of life, the engraving furnishes valuable material for studying the music, dancing and variety shows of the Han Dynasty.

Economic and Cultural Exchanges with Foreign Countries

A new situation emerged in economic and cultural exchanges with foreign countries during the Han Dynasty. Zhang Qian went to the Western Regions on two occasions as an imperial envoy, opening up a land route from Chang'an, the capital, to Central and Western Asia through the Hexi corridor (corridor west of the Yellow River) and along the southern road of the Tianshan Range. Through this land route, the exquisitely-made silk of the Han empire found its way to countries in the West, and in return goods from the West were introduced into the Han empire. This was the famous Silk Road, the opening of which enhanced cultural intercourse between the Han empire and its neighbors, and enriched the life of the people in both the East and the West.

257. Communications of the Han Dynasty with Foreign Countries The Han Dynasty saw new developments in China's foreign relations. Zhang Qian's two trips to the Western Regions opened a line of communication, later known as the "Silk Road," between China and several countries of Central and West Asia.The Han empire also established friendly relations with its neighboring countries and charted sea routes to facilitate economic and cultural exchange with the outside world.

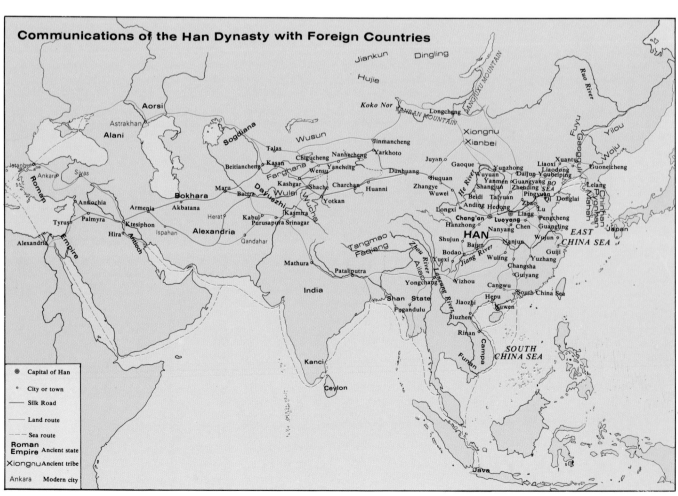

Communications of the Han Dynasty with Foreign Countries

258. Lead coin with inscriptions in ancient Greek Foreign currency, 5.5 cm in diameter, 0.9 cm thick, weight 115.45 g,Eastern Han; unearthed in 1979 at Xiamenxiang, Pingliang, Gansu Province. One side of the coin bears a raised bird design, while the other side is concave and has a circle of inscriptions in ancient Greek. Several hundred similar lead and copper coins were unearthed at Han sites in Xi'an and Fufeng, Shaanxi Province, and in Lingtai, Gansu Province. Archaeologists believe they were foreign coins circulated into China from the Western Regions. The inscriptions contain mistakes in ancient Greek, made probably in copying the words.

259. Yutian (Khotan) coin with inscriptions in two languages 2.4 cm in diameter, 0.4 cm thick, weight 14.9 g, Eastern Han; unearthed north of Hotan, Xinjiang Uygur Autonomous Region, in 1929. The front side of the coin bears a circle of Chinese characters in the seal style meaning "copper coin weighing 24 *zhu*," and the reverse side, the image of a walking horse surrounded by 20 words in Kharosthi. Both the inscriptions and design were made by die casting, a traditional Greek method of minting widely adopted by the countries of Central Asia. The ancient Yutian State, bordering on the northwest of South Asia and the east of West Asia, once spoke the Kharosthi language. When the Han empire opened a line of communication with the Western Regions, it had close trade relations with the Yutian State, and the latter began using Chinese on the coins it minted.

258

259

260. Green glass cup Beverage vessel, 3.4 cm high, 5.9 cm in diameter, Eastern Han; unearthed in 1955 in Guixian, Guangxi Zhuang Autonomous Region. Made by die pressing and polishing, this cup was originally pale green and transparent, the surface having turned black through weathering. A chemical analysis shows that it was made of soda-lime glass, with the same component parts as Roman glass. This vessel bears witness to the early economic and cultural exchanges between the Han Dynasty and the Western countries.

260

261. Blue glass bowl Beverage vessel, 4.7 cm high, rim 10.5 cm in diameter, Western Han; unearthed in 1954 at Hengzhigang, Guangzhou, Guangdong Province. This is the earliest Roman glass vessel unearthed in China.Dark bluish violet in color, it was made by die pressing, while the outer surface and the rim were ground. The bow-string intaglio pattern under the rim was roughly ground. Archaeologists consider it to be a bowl produced in a center of Roman glass-making in the southern region of the Mediterranean, during the first century BC.

261

Three Kingdoms through Western and Eastern Jin to Northern and Southern Dynasties

(AD 220-589)

The collapse of the Eastern Jin Dynasty ushered in a period of over 300 years of disunity, covering the epochs of the Three Kingdoms, Western and Eastern Jin, and Northern and Southern Dynasties. During this period, with a further concentration of landholdings and the migration to the Central Plains of many ethnic minorities, class and national contradictions became very acute, and wars broke out frequently. Short-lived dynasties ruled one after another, and often several regimes existed side by side. In the north various nationalities fused with each other in the course of their activities, promoting economic revival and development, while in the south large numbers of migrants from the north worked cooperatively with the original inhabitants, helping to achieve a rapid development of the economy. Despite the split of China into northern and southern dynasties, the various regions and nationalities in the country maintained close ties, with the Central Plains as the

center, and had frequent economic and cultural exchanges with foreign countries. This laid the foundation for reunification later and a flourishing economy and culture under the Sui and Tang.

Confrontation between Wei, Shu and Wu

The Yellow Turban uprising shook the Eastern Han regime to its foundations, seriously weakening its rule. Many county and prefecture officials and big landlords developed into warlords; they raised armies, built castles, seized power in different parts of the country, and waged incessant wars. Cao Cao succeeded in wiping out most of the northern warlords, bringing the entire Yellow River valley under his control. Liu Bei and Sun Quan seized the vast territories in the southwest and southeast. In 220 Cao Pi, Cao Cao's eldest son, dethroned the Han emperor and established the kingdom of Wei, making Luoyang his capital. In 221 Liu Bei proclaimed himself emperor of Shu with Chengdu as his capital, and in 229 Sun Quan made himself emperor of Wu and moved his capital to Jianye (now Nanjing, Jiangsu Province). Thus the country was divided into three independent kingdoms.

262. Sketch Map Showing the Confrontations between the Three Kingdoms Cao Cao, battling in the name of the Han emperor, successively eliminated the forces of Lü Bu, Yuan Shao and Liu Biao and built up his political and military strength in north China. In 208 he led an army of 200,000 southward to attack Liu Bei and pose a direct menace to Sun Quan. At Chibi, on the middle reaches of the Yangtze River, however, Cao Cao's army suffered a disastrous defeat at the hands of the 60,000 allied forces of Sun Quan and Liu Bei and was driven back north. After that Sun Quan consolidated his economic and military position in the middle and lower reaches of the Yangtze River, while Liu Bei seized the vast area in southwest China. Thus the Three Kingdoms were established, with the Wu, ruled by the house of Sun, and the Shu, ruled by the house of Liu, joining hands and relying on the favorable terrain in south China against Wei, ruled by the house of Cao.

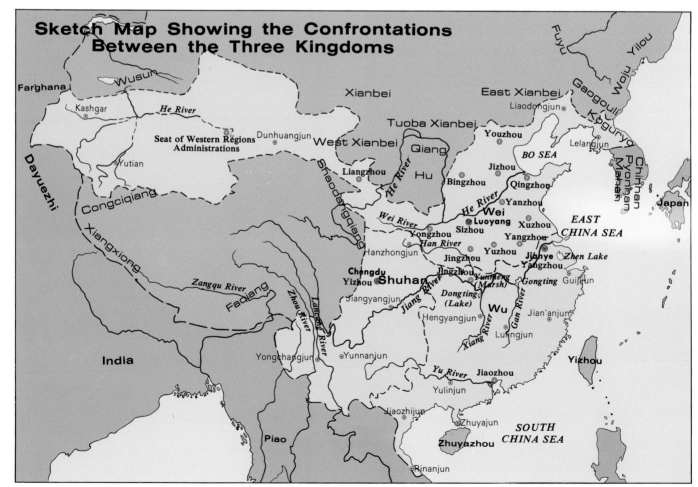

263

263. *Wuzhu* coin Wei currency, 2.5 cm in diameter, weight 3.4–3.5 g, Three Kingdoms Period. Cereals in the Han Dynasty normally sold at 30 to 100-odd *wuzhu* coins a *dan* or a *hu* (approx. 20 liters). With the currency collapsing at the end of the dynasty, their prices soared to many thousand and even over a million *wuzhu* coins a *dan* or a *hu*. Since the coins became almost worthless, trade by barter prevailed. After the Wei unified north China, Emperor Cao Pi issued a decree in 221 ordering that the use of *wuzhu* coins be resumed. The decree, however, was abolished half a year later because prices were still very high. It was not until 227, during the reign of Emperor Cao Rui, that *wuzhu* coins were put to use again, an indication that economic life had returned to normal by then.

264. Pottery cup with side ears Wine cup, c. 11 cm long, Wei of the Three Kingdoms; unearthed from the Cao Zhi tomb in Dong'e, Shandong Province. Cao Zhi, son of Cao Cao, had great talent for literature. Because of his indiscreet behavior and heavy drinking, he lost the chance to succeed his father on the throne and died a bitter and disappointed man.

264

265-1

265. Bronze mirror with immortal-and-animal motif Wei relic of the Three Kingdoms, 15 cm in diameter; unearthed in 1987 in Luoyang, Henan Province. This mirror is decorated mainly with relief images of immortals and animals such as dragons and tigers. Mirrors of this kind first appeared in the mid Eastern Han and continued to be in vogue up to the Three Kingdoms Period.

266

266. Bronze trigger mechanism of a crossbow Weapon, 11.9 cm long, Wei of the Three Kingdoms. Crossbows were a light weapon that had been widely used since pre-Qin days. The one in the picture was made in 241, the second year of the Zhengshi reign of Wei, when the three kingdoms of Wei, Shu and Wu were locked in fighting. At the end of the Three Kingdoms Period, China had a population of about 16 million, of which the Wu numbered 2.3 millions, the Shu numbered 940,000, and the Wei (later Western Jin), the most powerful of the three, made up three quarters.

265-2

267

267. *Zhibai wuzhu* coin Shu currency, 2.6-2.8 cm in diameter, weight 3-9.5 g, Three Kingdoms Period. In 213 Liu Bei took Chengdu, making it the political center of Shu. The state treasury being depleted, the Shu issued a *zhibai wuzhu* coin, which was worth 100 *wuzhu* coins but only a little over twice the weight of the latter. At the same time, it took measures to curb inflation and opened state-administered trade markets. The state coffers of Shu filled in just a few months.

268. Pottery figurine with a dustpan Funerary object, 54 cm high, Shu of the Three Kingdoms; unearthed in 1981 in Zhongxian, Sichuan Province. The figurine depicts a woman working with a dustpan. In the 3rd-6th centuries (from the Three Kingdoms Period to the Northern and Southern Dynasties) large numbers of freemen became servants to the landlord class and powerful families. The figurine is a portrayal of just such a servant.

268

269. Bronze mirror with immortal-and-animal motif Wu relic of the Three Kingdoms, 12 cm in diameter. This mirror was made in 262, the fifth year of the Yong'an reign of the Wu emperor Jingdi (Sun Xiu). Southeast China, where the Wu regime was located, was noted for its rich deposits of copper in ancient times. Guiji Prefecture was a center for making bronze mirrors from the mid Eastern Han to the Three Kingdoms Period. Most the workshops that turned out exquisite bronze mirrors were privately run, and their mirrors were decorated on the back, usually with an immortal-and-animal motif, sometimes with portraits of historical figures.

270-1

270. Celadon lamp   11.5 cm high, Wu of the Three Kingdoms; unearthed in 1958 in Nanjing, Jiangsu Province. A lamp in a novel shape, it features a bear cub, as charmingly naive as a child, carrying the oil plate on the head. Engraved on the bottom of the lamp are seven characters meaning "Made in the fifth month of the first year of the Ganlu reign." That was the year AD 265.

271. Lion-shaped celadon water dropper   Container of water for an inkslab, 12.6 cm long, Wu of the Three Kingdoms; unearthed in 1958 in Nanjing, Jiangsu Province. Iron as a coloring agent in glaze exists in two forms: ferrous oxide, which gives a green color, and ferric oxide, which produces dark brown or terra-cotta. The water dropper in the picture, a celadon gem of the Three Kingdoms Period, is in the shape of a fierce lion coated with grayish-green glaze.

271

270-2

272. Sheep-shaped celadon *zun* Water vessel, 30.5 cm long, 25 cm high, Wu of the Three Kingdoms; unearthed in 1958 in Nanjing, Jiangsu Province. In the Yangtze Delta, an area rich in kaolin, porcelain-making technology had basically matured by the mid and late Eastern Han, and was further improved in the Three Kingdoms Period, when porcelain was made on a fairly large scale. The *zun* in the picture, in the shape of a meek sheep and evenly-coated with a lustrous glaze, represents the highest level of porcelain making at the time.

273. Pottery courtyard house

Funerary object, 54 cm long, 44 cm wide, Wu of the Three Kingdoms; unearthed in 1967 in Ezhou, Hubei Province. Modeled on a real building, this pottery courtyard house, surrounded by a wall, has a room for receiving guests in the front, a main room facing south at the back, and side rooms on the east and west. Built in the wall are a front gate with a tower above it, a back gate, and four corner towers; all the towers serve as sentry posts. Engraved on the tower above the gate are seven characters meaning "General Sun's Gate Tower." The pottery house, therefore, was probably modeled on the residence of Sun Shu, a member of the royal family of Wu and military commander of Wuchang (present-day E'zhou), a city of strategic importance and twice the capital of the Kingdom of Wu. Wu moved its capital to Jianye (now Nanjing) later.

274. Pottery *dui*

Funerary object, 13 cm long, 3.9 cm wide, Wu of the Three Kingdoms; unearthed in 1958 in Nanjing, Jiangsu Province. The *dui* was a mortar and pestle for husking grain in ancient China. A *dui* in actual use consisted of a long piece of wood with a hollow at one end where the grain to be husked was put. A treadle-operated wooden tilt hammer, fixed with a heavy head, was propped up over it.

274

273

Western Jin's Brief Unification

In 263 Wei conquered Shu. Two years later Sima Yan forced the Wei emperor to abdicate and set up the Jin Dynasty (historically known as the Western Jin), with the capital remaining at Luoyang as during the Wei. In 280 Jin conquered Wu, the last of the Three Kingdoms, reuniting the country. Representing the interests of great families, the Western Jin government allowed peasants to own a certain amount of farmland and levied a tax on it, maintained the system of "nine official grades," and granted the title of prince to members of the royal family. After the death of Sima Yan large-scale internecine wars, known as the "Disturbances of the Eight Princes," broke out, followed by uprisings of refugees and migrant ethnic minorities. Liu Yuan and Liu Yao, two Xiongnu nobles, occupied Luoyang in 311 and Chang'an in 316, ending the short-lived Western Jin.

275. Bronze seal carved with the characters "Qin Jin Hu Wang"
About 2.5 cm long on each side, Western Jin. This seal was conferred on an ethnic minority leader in north China by the Western Jin government.

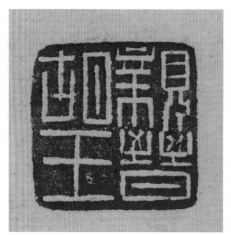

275-1

275-2

276. Pottery figurines of swordsmen Funerary objects, left 20 cm high, right 17 cm high, Western Jin; unearthed in Changsha, Hunan Province. Families of power and influence in the Western Jin, as at the end of the Han, owned large numbers of armed men known as *buqu*. Interment of clay figurines of the *buqu*, such as the ones in the picture, in the tombs of these families showed the high standing of the tomb occupants.

277. Pottery figurines of horsemen Funerary objects, 22-24 cm high, Western Jin; unearthed in Changsha, Hunan Province. Altogether 29 figurines were unearthed from a tomb in Changsha. Twenty-three of them, including the seven in the picture, are of a guard of honor. One of the seven horsemen plays a wind instrument, and the others each carry a wooden slip. The guard of honor was a symbol of official rank at the time; the higher the rank, the more men in the guard of honor.

278

279

278. Iron halberds   Weapons, remaining parts 16.8 cm (left) and 23 cm (right) long, Western Jin; unearthed in 1953 from the Zhou Chu tomb in Yixing, Jiangsu Province. Zhou Chu did all kinds of bad things when he was young, and was referred to as one of three evils, the other two being the flood dragon and the beast of prey. Later he turned over a new leaf, seeking fame and honor and unafraid of influential officials. In 297, when a severe drought struck northwest China, the People of Di and Qiang, two ethnic minorities, stirred up a turmoil there. Zhou Chu led an army of 5,000 against the Di and Qiang troops, who totalled 70,000, and was killed in action.

279. Celadon incense burner   19.5 cm high, Western Jin; unearthed in 1953 in Yixing, Jiangsu Province. In the 3rd-6th centuries (from the Three Kingdoms Period to the Northern and Southern Dynasties) the nobility liked to burn incense to remove disagreeable odors. Shi Hu, a minister of the Later Zhao, set gold incense burners around the bed-curtain in his room, and Xiao Baojuan, Emperor of Qi of the Southern Dynasties, covered the floor with musk, trying to please his favorite concubine. During the Southern Dynasties young civilian officials always wore clothes that gave off a sweet smell, while high-ranking ladies on a journey would be followed by people carrying incense burners. Various aromatic substances, some from foreign countries, were available at the time.

280. Porcelain male and female figurines
Funerary objects, female 23.5 cm high, male 20.5 cm high, Western Jin; unearthed in 1964 in Nanjing, Jiangsu Province.The female figurine, stripped to the waist, probably portrays a slave. In the 3rd-6th centuries (from the Three Kingdoms Period to the Northern and Southern Dynasties) large numbers of people were reduced to slavery. Criminals' families were made slaves and placed under the control of local authorities. However, slaves owned by individuals far exceeded the government-owned ones in number; some families had as many as several thousand slaves. Prisoners of war were often distributed as slaves to meritorious officials; impoverished people would also sell themselves as slaves. Slaves in a family did various kinds of work: farming, trading, handiwork and family chores. The male figurine, looking like a child, is dressed in the costume of a *li* (a runner in a *yamen*). The *li*, whose status was lower than that of the common people, were selected from people in the 13-60, sometimes even 8-80, age group.

Further Exploitation of the South

The Eastern Jin and the four regimes (Song, Qi, Liang and Chen) collectively known as the Southern Dynasties ruled south China from 317 to 589. Wholesale migration from the north brought with it more advanced techniques of production to the south, and increasingly closer ties between the Han people and various southern nationalities led to further exploitation of the resources of south China. Great developments were made in the handicraft industries such as silk weaving, smelting and founding, and in the making of celadon and paper, as well as in commerce, transportation and communication.

Rule of Eastern Jin in the South

In 318, with the support of great families, Sima Rui proclaimed himself emperor of Eastern Jin, making Jiankang (now Nanjing, Jiangsu Province) his capital. A fierce struggle for land and power rose within the Eastern Jin ruling clique. Meanwhile, in the north, the Former Qin established by the Di nationality became strong and it began to covet the territory of Eastern Jin. In 383, however, its army suffered a serious setback in the Battle of Feishui and its plans for conquest had to be abandoned. This resulted in a long-term division between north and south China, a situation that proved favorable to the economic development in the south.

281. Pottery figurine of a woman
Funerary object, 33.7 cm high,
Eastern Jin; unearthed in Nanjing,
Jiangsu Province. The figurine
depicts a maidservant watching
something with an amused
expression on her face.

281-1

Quick Succession of Song, Qi, Liang and Chen

The end of Eastern Jin was followed by the quick succession of Song, Qi, Liang and Chen, established by Liu Yu, Xiao Daocheng, Xiao Yan and Chen Baxian in 420, 479, 502 and 557 respectively. They all had their capital at Jiankang.

282

282. Celadon amphora with chicken-head spout   Wine vessel, 22.3 cm high, Southern Dynasties; unearthed in 1965 in Zhenjiang, Jiangsu Province. This vessel is succinct in both shape and design. During the Western and Eastern Jin and Northern and Southern Dynasties, many celebrated scholars were addicted to drinking, which is why wine vessels are often found in tombs of that period.

283. Celadon cup and saucer   Tea set, saucer c. 16 cm in diameter, cup c. 12 cm in diameter, Southern Dynasties; unearthed in Fuzhou, Fujian Province. In the period from the Han to the Southern Dynasties people liked to drink boiled tea, known as *zhoucha*. Green Chinese onion, ginger, dates, orange peel, dogwood or peppermint were sometimes boiled with tea leaves.

284. Celadon *zun* with lotus flower motif
Water or wine vessel, 49.5 cm high, Southern Dynasties; unearthed in Shangcai, Henan Province. Buddhism was widely propagated in China during the Northern and Southern Dynasties, when many buildings and articles for daily use were decorated with Buddhist images. The *zun* pictured here is a magnificent vessel with a neck featuring two flying devas and four Buddhas sitting cross-legged, and a belly decorated with three circles of relief sculptures of lotus flowers facing downward while one circle of lotus flowers faces upward. Deva means a deity in Buddhism. A score of devas, many of them flying devas, so named because they are depicted in a flying posture, are mentioned in Buddhist scriptures. As disciples and bodyguards of the Buddha, flying devas play music, scatter flowers, and uphold karmic law. Lotus flowers symbolize purity in Buddhism.

283

Economic Development in the South

As large numbers of northerners moved to the south to escape the chaos caused by war in the late Western Jin, they brought with them north China's advanced tools and techniques of production. During this period south China witnessed great development in agriculture, with large amounts of wasteland reclaimed, many irrigation works built and farming techniques much improved. Handicrafts, too, flourished. Over the next few centuries the vast areas south of the Yangtze River became rich and prosperous.

285. Celadon sheepfold Funerary object, 9.8 cm in diameter, Jin Dynasty. Models of pigsties, sheepfolds, and chicken and duck coops were often interred in tombs as funerary objects in the 3rd-6th centuries (from the Three Kingdoms Period to the Northern and Southern Dynasties). Many such funerary objects were unearthed in the Yangtze Delta. They reflect the manorial economy prevailing at the time.

286. Celadon pigsty Funerary object, 10 cm in diameter, Jin Dynasty. Models like this were found often in tombs of the Three Kingdoms and the Jin in the Yangtze Delta.

285

286

287. Black porcelain amphora with chicken-head spout Wine vessel, 15.6 cm high, Eastern Jin; unearthed in Zhenjiang, Jiangsu Province. Porcelain coated with dark brown or black glaze is known as black porcelain. Dark brown porcelain first appeared in the late Eastern Han. The amphora in the picture shows the technical maturity in making black porcelain. The main coloring agent in both black porcelain and celadon is iron, which reaches 4-8% in the glaze of the former and no more than 3% in that of the latter.

288. Sheep-shaped celadon candle holder   17 cm long, 14.7 cm high, Eastern Jin; unearthed in Zhenjiang, Jiangsu Province. A grayish green vessel with dark brown spots, this two-color candle holder was made by adding a little dark brown glaze substance to the grayish green glaze before firing at a high temperature.

289. Ten-legged celadon inkslab
Writing article, 13.4 cm in diameter, 4.7 cm high, Southern Dynasties; unearthed in 1960 in Zhenjiang, Jiangsu Province. Inkslabs were first made of stone. Porcelain inkslabs did not appear until the Western Jin. The celadon inkslab in the

289

288-2

picture has glazed legs and outside surface, and rough, unglazed inside surface for rubbing ink. Made in various shapes and colors, porcelain inkslabs are much more beautiful than stone ones.

290. Celadon spittoon with stamped decoration   12 cm high, Southern Dynasties; unearthed in 1954 in Changsha, Hunan Province. In the 3rd-6th centuries (from the Three Kingdoms Period to the Northern and Southern Dynasties) people in China used to sit on a low bed, with a spittoon beside it. The yellowish green spittoon in the picture, shiny and smooth, is a gem of Southern Dynasties porcelain.

◁ 288-1

290

Amalgamation of Nationalities in the North

The fall of Western Jin in 316 was followed by the emergence of sixteen states existing side by side. In 439 Northern Wei unified north China, a unity that lasted nearly 100 years until 534 when it split into the Eastern and Western Wei. Later, these two states were replaced by Northern Qi and Northern Zhou respectively. In 577 Northern Zhou conquered Northern Qi and the north was again united. The various nationalities in north China, through long periods of productive activities and living together, gradually fused with each other, resulting in a flourishing economy. By the Sui Dynasty north China had become more powerful, and in 589 Sui conquered Chen, the last of the Southern Dynasties, ending the 300-year division between north and south.

Rise and Fall of the Sixteen States

North China was rent with disunity after the fall of Western Jin. Many ethnic minorities entered the Central Plains with their armies and set up independent regimes. Over a period of some 100 years, until reunification in 439 by Northern Wei, more than 20 states were established by the Han, Xiongnu, Xianbei, Jie, Di and Qiang nationalities. Sixteen of the states were prominent, namely Chen Han, Former Zhao, Later Zhao, Former Qin, Later Qin, Western Qin, Former Yan, Later Yan, Southern Yan, Northern Yan, Former Liang, Later Liang, Southern Liang, Northern Liang, Western Liang and Xia. Historically, this period is known as the Sixteen States.

291

292

293

291. ***Daxia Zhenxing*** **coin** Xia currency, 2.3 cm in diameter, weight 2.2 g. The Xia, a regime of the Xiongnu nationality in northwest China, was one of the sixteen states set up in the country between 304 and 409. Founded by Helian Bobo, the Xia lasted only 25 years. Zhenxing was the reign title of Helian Bobo after he proclaimed himself emperor of Xia.

292. ***Hanxing*** **coin** Cheng Han currency, 1.67 cm in diameter, weight 0.7-1.1 g. The Cheng Han, one of the earliest of the sixteen states, was founded by Li Xiong of the Di nationality. The later period of the Western Jin regime saw refugees and immigrants of ethnic minorities rising in one rebellion after another. Li Xiong, leader of over a hundred thousand refugees from northwest China, defeated the army of Western Jin in Chengdu and established the Kingdom of Cheng, also known as Cheng Han, in southwest China.

293. ***Taiqingfengle*** **and** ***Liangzaoxinquan*** **coins** Former Liang currency, 2.2 and 2.05 cm in diameter respectively. The Former Liang, one of the sixteen states, was set up in northwest China following disturbances in the Western Jin. Ruled by a line of Han monarchs surnamed Zhang, it belonged to the Western Jin in name only. To escape from war, many people from the interior of the country migrated to northwest China during the later period of the Western Jin, contributing to the rapid development of the economy and culture there and the smashing of many attacks by the armies of Former Zhao and Later Zhao. The Former Liang minted coins to replace cloth that had been used in trade by barter in the area.

294. ***Shi'an Hanchou*** **brick** Building material, 15.5 cm long, Later Zhao; unearthed in 1954 in Xi'an, Shaanxi Province. The Later Zhao, one of the sixteen states, was founded by Shi Le of the Jie nationality. Shi Le was originally an official in the state of Zhao ruled by the House of Liu, but later established his own state of Zhao. To differentiate the two, historians call Shi Le's state Later Zhao and the other Former Zhao. The Later Zhao made Xiangguo (now Xingtai, Hebei Province) the capital. When the state was in its prime, it occupied most of north China. Shi'an was the name of a county belonging to the Later Zhao in northwest China, and Hanchou, the name of the artisan who made the brick. Shi Le appointed Han people as officials, set up schools, made laws, and adopted the tax policy of the Three Kingdoms and the Western Jin that was acceptable to the Han people.

294

295

295. Eaves tile with characters "Da Qin Long Xing Hua Mou Gu Sheng"   Building material, 17.5 cm in diameter, Former Qin; unearthed in Yixian, Hebei Province. The Former Qin, one of the sixteen states, was set up by the Di nationality. Fu Jian, the third emperor of the Former Qin, unified north China, took the western area of the Eastern Jin, and brought the Western Regions (now Xinjiang Uygur Autonomous Region) under control. He set political standards for his officials, started courses on the teachings of Confucius, and fostered a prosperous economy. The characters on the eaves tile in the picture, a tile probably for use in an official residence, sing the praises of the Former Qin, saying that its exploits were comparable to those of a sage.

296. Stone dagoba built by Bai Shuangjie   Structure with Buddhist images for one to watch while meditating, remaining part 46 cm high, 21 cm in diameter at the bottom, Northern Liang; unearthed in Jiuquan, Gansu Province. The Northern Liang, one of the sixteen states, was founded by Juqu Mengxun, leader of an ethnic minority that inhabited the Lushui area in northwest China. Juqu Mengxun, a believer in Buddhism, loved the Han culture and liked to employ people of talent of the Han nationality. After the Northern Liang was conquered by the Northern Wei, large numbers of its artisans were brought to Pingcheng, capital of the Northern Wei, to build Buddhist temples and sculpt Buddhist statues. The Northern Liang thus became an intermediary through which Buddhist art spread from the west to the interior of the country. Bai Shuangjie, the builder of the stone dagoba, was a lay Buddhist of the Northern Liang.

296

297

Unification of the North by Northern Wei

In the mid third century the Tuoba clan of the Xianbei tribe moved from the Greater Xing'an range to the area around Shengle (north of present-day Horinger, Inner Mongolia Autonomous Region). In 315 the Western Jin emperor made Yilu, chief of the Tuoba clan, Prince of Dai. In 386 Tuoba Gui set up the state of Wei (historically known as Northern Wei), making Pingcheng (now Datong, Shanxi Province) his capital. During the reign of Tuoba Tao, the Northern Wei became very powerful and unified the entire Yellow River valley.

298

297. Eaves tile carved "Chuan Zuo Wu Qiong"   Building material, 15.5 cm in diameter, Northern Wei; unearthed in Datong, Shanxi Province. The four characters on the eaves title express the wish of the Northern Wei rulers to perpetuate their rule eternally. Many such tiles were unearthed in Datong, which was known as Pingcheng when it served as capital of the Northern Wei between 398 and 493.

298. Bronze caldron with circular base   Cooking vessel, 19.5 cm high, Northern Wei; unearthed in 1961 in Tumd Banner, Inner Mongolia Autonomous Region. A cooking vessel habitually used by nomadic people in north China, this caldron has two ears on the rim for tying a rope so that it could hang from a frame when cooking. Vessels of this shape were in use before the Christian Era, across an extensive area from Eastern Europe to north China. We may call it a typical example of the cultural exchange between east and west along the Silk Road.

299

299. Bronze plate with bird motif

Pendant, 5.5 cm long, Northern Wei; unearthed in 1961 in Tumd Banner, Inner Mongolia Autonomous Region. In ancient times bronze plates with images of animals or human beings were favorite ornaments used in belts, on harnesses or elsewhere by the Xiongnu, Wuhuan and Xianbei tribes in north China. The Xianbei tribe at first inhabited the northernmost part of that region. Later it moved westward and southward and for a time occupied all the grasslands in north China. Around the 3rd or 4th century the Tuoba clan of the Xianbei tribe settled down in what is now the middle part of the Inner Mongolia Autonomous Region. The bronze plate pictured was owned by a magistrate of Henei Prefecture in the interior of the country. After he died, his body was brought back and buried in his native place.

300. Bronze ruler

Measuring tool, 30.9 cm long, Northern Wei. The standard ruler in the Han Dynasty was 23-24 centimeters long. Two hundred years later, in the Eastern Jin, the ruler became one centimeter longer. After 100 more years, while a standard 25-centimeter ruler was used in the Southern Dynasties, the ruler in the Northern Wei was nearly 31 centimeters long. This was because the Northern Wei government levied taxes in kind, and increasing the length, capacity and weight in the measuring tools meant an increase in revenues.

300

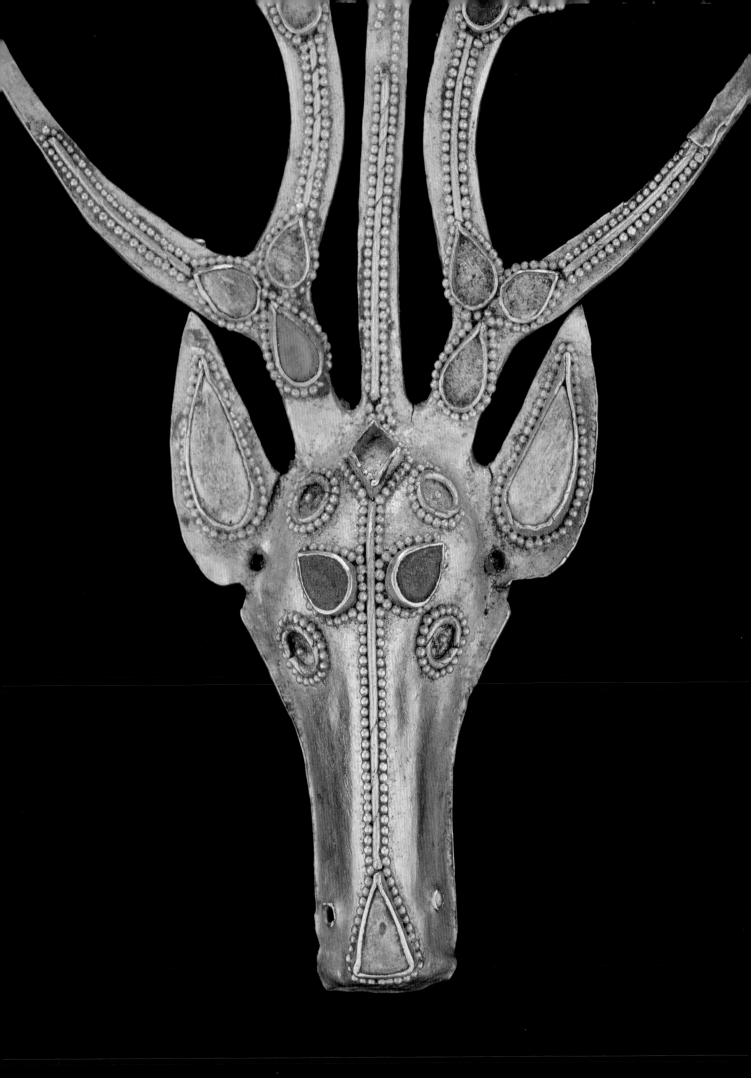

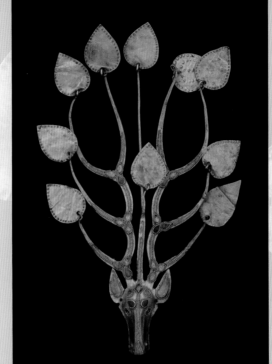

301-2

302

301. Horse head with antlers

302. Ox head with antlers Gold headdresses, 16.2 and 17.5 cm high and weight c. 70 and 90 g respectively, Northern Dynasties; unearthed in 1981 in Damao Banner, Inner Mongolia Autonomous Region. These headdresses, known as *buyao*, were designed for the upper-level nobility of the Xianbei nationality. Animal-shaped ornaments, it was believed, could exorcise evil spirits and bring happiness. The ornament wearers, walking with the antlers' leaf blades swaying, looked stately and graceful.

◁ 301-1

304

303. Mounted warriors (clay figurines)

Funerary objects, 38 cm high, Northern Wei; unearthed in 1953 from the Caochangpo tomb in Xi'an, Shaanxi Province. These clay figurines of armor-clad warriors and horses show the Xianbei soldiers' usual way of fighting on horseback. The Northern Wei, a regime set up by the Tuoba clan of the Xianbei tribe, retained much of the Xianbei customs and traits in its early period. In 493, the 17th year of the Taihe reign of Emperor Xiaowen, the Northern Wei carried out reforms that resulted in the quick assimilation by the Xianbei of Han culture. The clay figurines in the picture were made with primitive pottery technique before the reform.

304. Beating a drum (clay figurine)

Funerary object, 29 cm high, Northern Wei; unearthed in 1953 from the Caochangpo tomb in Xi'an, Shaanxi Province. Altogether 60 figurines of a guard of honor were retrieved from the tomb. Six of the figurines represent a *guchui* group:three persons beating drums, one beating a gong, and two blowing clarionets. In the Northern Wei the emperor bestowed *guchui* groups only on high-ranking officials. An official with a large retinue on a journey would look and sound impressive and dignified with the beating of drums and gongs and the blare of clarionets coming from both the head and the rear of the procession.

305-1

305. Women singer and musicians (clay figurines)   Funerary objects, musicians playing the zither 22.5 cm high, singer 24 cm high, Northern Wei; unearthed in 1953 from the Caochangpo tomb in Xi'an, Shaanxi Province. Figurines of a musician blowing the panpipes and one playing another wind instrument were also retrieved from the tomb. In the Northern Wei orchestras and singers were employed in the royal court and official mansions. In their performances the tunes were fixed, with the words written specially by the emperor or officials or coming from folk songs. The audience sometimes clapped hands to the rhythm of the music in a performance.

305-2

306. Tomb-guarding beast (clay sculpture)   Funerary object, 25.5 cm high, Northern Wei; unearthed in 1965 from the Yuan Shao tomb in Luoyang, Henan Province. Clay tomb-guarding beasts first appeared in the Western Jin. At first only one such sculpture stood at the entrance to a tomb. The number of sculptures increased to two in the Northern Wei and to four during the Tang.

306

307. Attendant (clay sculpture)

Funerary object, 17.7 cm high, Northern Wei; unearthed in 1965 from the Yuan Shao tomb in Luoyang, Henan Province. Yuan Shao, the tomb occupant, died in 528, over 20 years after Emperor Xiaowen had implemented his reforms. The sculpture reflects the changes in the hairstyle and dress of the attendant. Unlike the ethnic minority people in north China, who wore their hair down and folded their clothes to the left, the attendant is dressed in the costume of a Han official in south China, tying up the hair under a small cap and folding his coat to the right.

307

308-2

308-3

308. Warrior (clay sculpture)
Funerary object, 30.8 cm high,
Northern Wei; unearthed in 1965 from
the Yuan Shao tomb in Luoyang,
Henan Province. This sculpture was
made after Emperor Xiaowen's
reforms. It has more features of the
Han style and a much better form of
expression by comparison with the
figurines of warriors unearthed from
the Caochangpo tomb.

◁ 308-1

Reforms of Northern Wei Emperor Xiaowen

In 439 Emperor Taiwu (born Tuoba Tao) of Northern Wei unified north China. On the basis of this unification Emperor Xiaowen (Tuoba Hong) carried out a series of reforms ranging from politics and economy to customs and habits. Moving its capital to Luoyang, the Northern Wei further assimilated elements in Han culture and completed the transition of the Tuoba clan to a feudal state. As a result, the economy in the north revived and developed.

309. Bronze seals carved "Guanjunjiangjun Yin," "Gaochenghou Yin," and "Huaizhoucishi Yin"   Each 3.5 cm long and 3 cm wide, Northern Wei; unearthed in 1948 from the Feng tomb in Jingxian, Hebei Province. The characters on the seals indicate the official position, military appointment and rank of nobility enjoyed by Feng Monu, the tomb occupant, during his lifetime. The house of Feng was a distinguished family from the Han to the Northern Dynasties.

310. Standing clay figure   Funerary object, 27.3 cm high, Northern Dynasties; unearthed in 1948 from the Feng tomb in Jingxian, Hebei Province. This figure portrays an attendant wearing a broad-sleeved gown with a black gauze hood, which was no different from the dress of Han officials in the Southern Dynasties.

311. Standing clay figure   Funerary object, 22.9 cm high, Northern Dynasties; unearthed in 1948 from the Feng tomb in Jingxian, Hebei Province. This is of a tall, sturdy warrior wearing a coat with the neck widely opened, which makes it convenient to remove one sleeve, exposing the arm and chest or the undergarments, a custom among the Xianbei people.

309

310

311

312

312. Standing clay figure Funerary object, 23 cm high, Northern Dynasties; unearthed in 1948 from the Feng tomb in Jingxian, Hebei Province. This represents a warrior wearing a cape with a hood, a costume of the ethnic minorities in north China. On the other hand, the image also looks like a dainty little girl with its full cheeks, round nose, small mouth and soft hands. This reflects the assimilation of the Xianbei into Han culture. The trend of making male figures with female features continued up to the early Tang Dynasty.

313. Epitaph for Yuan Yu Stone square tomb tablet, 55.2 cm long, 51.6 cm wide, 16.4 cm thick, Northern Wei; unearthed in Luoyang, Henan Province. The inscription on the tablet gives a brief account of the life and family status of Yuan Yu, a younger brother of Emperor Xiaowen (born Yuan Hong). When the emperor moved the capital to Luoyang, Yuan Yu, by imperial order, stayed in

313

Pingcheng, the old capital, to control and appease a number of Xianbei people who opposed the move of capital. One of the reforms made by Emperor Xiaowen was the change of the surnames and places of origin of the Xianbei people. The royal house of Xianbei, for instance, was originally surnamed Tuoba. *Tuo* in the Xianbei language means land, the origin of

"ten thousand things of creation;" *ba* means a monarch. This was changed to Yuan, a character that in the Han language has a similar meaning. Their place origin was changed to Luoyang.

314. Clay horse Funerary object, 31.3 cm high, Northern Dynasties; unearthed in 1948 from the Feng tomb in Jingxian, Hebei Province. As a component of the guard of honor, clay horses were found in all the tombs of the nobility of this period.

314

315

315. Civil and military officials (clay figures)　Funerary objects, civil official 38.9 cm high, military official 40.2 cm high, Western Wei; unearthed in 1977 from a Western Wei tomb in Cuijiaying, Hanzhong, Shaanxi Province. The clay figures retrieved from this tomb are similar in appearance to the images in Western Wei murals and sculptures in cave 285 of the Mogao Grottoes in Dunhuang, Gansu Province. Dressed in loose coats with wide girdles, they all have delicate features and look natural and unaffected.

316. Musician playing the *pipa* (clay figure)　Funerary object, 28.2 cm high, Northern Qi; unearthed in 1973 from the Kudi Huiluo tomb in Shouyang, Shanxi Province. Kudi Huiluo was a high-ranking military officer of the Northern Qi. His tomb was in the form of an early timber structure, decorated with gorgeous murals. The clay figure pictured is just one of many beautiful funerary objects found in the tomb. An exquisite item of its kind, it portrays a well-dressed musician with a dignified expression on his face.

Eastern Wei, Western Wei, Northern Qi and Northern Zhou

Political corruption coupled with an accelerating process of concentration of landholdings led to sharper social contradictions in the later period of Northern Wei, and finally to the division of the regime into Eastern and Western Wei. Yuan Shanjian, with the support of Gao Huan, became emperor of Eastern Wei with his capital at Yecheng (now Linzhang, Hebei Province) in 534, and the following year Yuan Baoju, with the support of Yuwen Tai, ascended the throne of Western Wei, making Chang'an his capital. In 550 Gao Yang, son of Gao Huan, deposed the Eastern Wei emperor and set up Northern Qi; in 557 Yuwen Jue, son of Yuwen Tai, did likewise in Western Wei, setting up Northern Zhou.

316-1

316-2 ▷

317. Pottery ox cart   Funerary object, cart 31.2 cm high, ox 23.2 cm high, Northern Qi; unearthed in 1955 from the Zhang Susu tomb in Kuangpo, Taiyuan, Shanxi Province. Retrieved from the tomb were pottery objects, such as the ox cart; *dui*, a treadle-operated tilt hammer for hulling rice; and millstones. All these objects reflect the life of the Han people. There were also pottery animals, such as camels, horses and sheep, which mirror the life of the ethnic minorities in north China. This shows that a cultural fusion of various nationalities took place at the time. The ox cart had been a means of transportation for members of the upper strata since the late Eastern Han. In the Northern Qi, when a nobleman and his followers went forth, the ox cart became the focus of attention in the procession.

318. Warriors (clay figures)   Funerary objects, c. 24 cm high, Northern Qi; unearthed in 1955 from the Zhang Susu tomb in Taiyuan, Shanxi Province. The images of the warriors are typical of people in north China: simple, honest and strong.

319. Clay camel   Funerary object, 29.8 cm high, 26.6 cm long, Northern Qi; unearthed in 1955 from the Zhang Susu tomb in Taiyuan, Shanxi Province. Camels were an important means of transportation in the desert. With the occupation of the Central Plains by the ethnic minorities of north China, clay camels began to appear in the Central Plains during the Northern Wei. They continued to be popular up to the Tang.

317

318

321

320. Yellow porcelain flask with figures of dancers and musicians Container, 20.5 cm high, rim 5.1 cm in diameter, circular base 10.1 cm in diameter, Northern Qi; unearthed in 1971 in Anyang, Henan Province. Identical figures of dancers and musicians were stamped on both sides of this oblate porcelain flask. The images and costumes of the figures suggest that they are the Hu (a general name of the northern tribes in ancient China) in the Western Regions. The dance they perform came from the ancient state of Tashkend in what is now the Tashkent area in Central Asia. Later, known as Hu Teng Dance, it became very popular during the Tang Dynasty.

321. Epitaph for Du Guxin Square stone tomb tablet, 41 cm on each side, 7.4 cm thick, Northern Zhou; unearthed in 1953 at Dizhangwan, Xianyang, Shaanxi Province. Du Guxin, a member of the Xianbei nationality, was a powerful senior general of Northern Zhou. Later, because of his involvement in opposition to Jin Gonghu, a minister regent, he was forced to commit suicide. Du's eldest daughter was the empress of Emperor Mingdi (born Yuwen Yu), and his seventh daughter was married to Yang Jian and later became Empress Wenxian when Yang Jian established the Sui Dynasty and proclaimed himself Emperor Wendi.

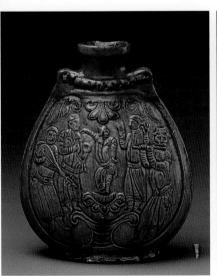

320-2

320-3

322

322. Eaves tile with lotus pattern Building material, 21.5 cm in diameter, Gaogouli; unearthed in 1976 in Ji'an, Jilin Province. Ji'an was the capital of Gaogouli, an ancient state in northeast China, between AD 3 and 427. The large number and great variety of Gaogouli eaves tiles unearthed in Ji'an provide important materials for studying the ancient state's palaces, tombs and other architecture. The lotus pattern on the tile,like similar decorations used in the Central Plains, symbolizes faith in Buddhism.

323. Gilded saddlebows and stirrups Harness articles, large saddlebow 50.5 cm wide, 29.8 cm high, small saddlebow 38 cm wide, 25.4 cm high, stirrups c. 26.8 cm high, c. 17.2 cm wide, Gaogouli; unearthed in 1976 in Ji'an, Jilin Province. Gilded Gaogouli articles possess distinctive local features. Most of them were harness articles; only a few were articles of personal adornment. Gaogouli's gold-plating technology, first introduced from the Central Plains, reached a high level in the fourth and fifth centuries, producing fine articles much enjoyed by the state's nobility and high-ranking military officers.

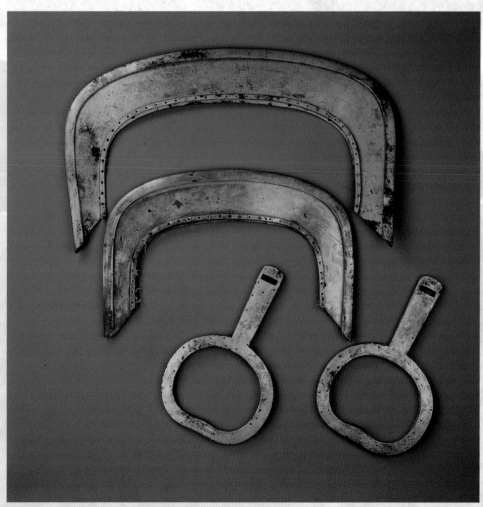

323

324. Yellow glazed pottery ewer Water or wine vessel, 33 cm high, rim 26 cm in diameter at the top and 12.6 at the bottom, Gaogouli; unearthed in 1963 in Ji'an, Jilin Province. Gaogouli glazed pottery vessels, unearthed in Ji'an, were made with the technology introduced from the Central Plains. They are, therefore, similar in shape to the glazed pottery of the Central Plains.

324

Cultural Exchange with Foreign Countries

China's trade and cultural ties with the West became closer during the 3rd-6th centuries (from the Three Kingdoms to the Northern and Southern Dynasties). Fa Xian, a monk of Eastern Jin, was the first to go west in search of Buddhist scriptures. He was also the first Chinese to travel along the Silk Road to countries of Central and South Asia and return to China by sea.

325. Route of Fa Xian's Journeys to and from the Buddhist Countries   Between AD 399 and 413 the Eastern Jin monk Fa Xian visited what are now Afghanistan, Pakistan, India, Nepal, Sri Lanka and Indonesia, searching for Buddhist scriptures and suffering untold hardships on the way. Setting out from Chang'an, he passed through the Hexi Corridor, climbed over the mountain ranges in west China, toured the South Asian Subcontinent, and returned to China by sea. The first Chinese to go abroad and then return by that route, Fa Xian brought back and translated into Chinese large numbers of Buddhist classics. In his book *A Record of the Buddhist Countries*, Fa Xian tells about the history, geography, religion, and customs of the countries in Central, South and Southeast Asia. It is a world-famous book on ancient history and geography.

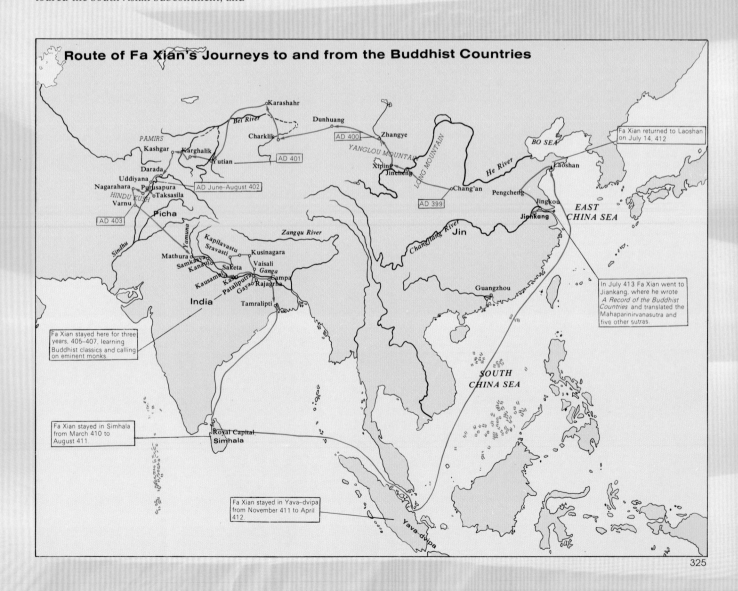

Route of Fa Xian's Journeys to and from the Buddhist Countries

Fa Xian returned to Laoshan on July 14, 412.

In July 413 Fa Xian went to Jiankang, where he wrote *A Record of the Buddhist Countries* and translated the Mahaparinirvanasutra and five other sutras.

Fa Xian stayed here for three years, 405–407, learning Buddhist classics and calling on eminent monks.

Fa Xian stayed in Simhala from March 410 to August 411.

Fa Xian stayed in Yava–dvipa from November 411 to April 412.

326

326. Silver flask Third-century
container, 15.8 cm high, rim 7 cm in
diameter at the top and 5.4 at the bottom;
unearthed at Shangsunjiazhai, Datong,
Qinghai Province. Altogether 182 tombs of
the Han-Jin period were excavated at
Shangsunjiazhai between 1973 and 1981.
The silver flask in the picture, unearthed
from a Jin tomb of a chief of the
Dongshuihu branch of the Xiongnu
nationality, is a third-century Roman
vessel made in what is now the area
around Syria, a vessel that bears witness
to China's long cultural and trade ties to
the West.

327

327. Gilded bronze goblet with inlaid decoration Wine vessel, 9.8 cm high, rim 11.2 cm in diameter, base 6.8 cm in diameter, Byzantium; unearthed in 1970 from a Northern Wei site on the outskirts of Datong, Shanxi Province. The modern city of Datong in Shanxi Province is where the capital of Northern Wei was located before it was moved to Luoyang in 494. In the fifth century, when the Northern Wei had economic and cultural ties with the West, quite a number of monks, artists and millinaire-type merchants from Central and West Asia lived in its capital. Many vessels rich in West Asian color in both shape and decor were retrieved from the Northern Wei site in Datong.

328. Glass cup with netlike pattern

Wine vessel, 6.7 cm high, rim 10.3 cm in diameter, base 4.5 cm in diameter, Byzantium; unearthed in 1948 from the Northern Wei cemetery of the house of Feng in Jingxian, Hebei Province. This cup, made by the glassblowing method, has very thin sides, measuring only 0.2 cm. It is smooth inside and has clear horizontal veins outside. A test shows that it was made of soda-lime glass. Archaeologists believe it is a legacy of the Eastern Roman Empire.

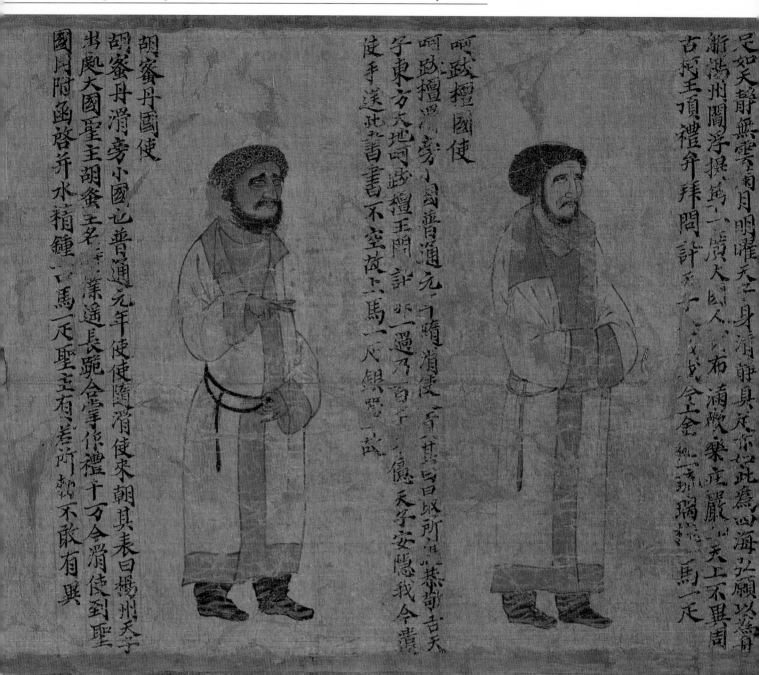

足如天靜無雲望而月明灌天之身清靜即具足亦宗如此為四海以願以為日
漸瀉州閻浮提為二質大因人二布涌歙樂痘嚴六天工不異周
古菸王頂禮弁拜問訃及十二戈文令工金　銘二斑瑙等二馬一疋

呵跋檀國使
呵跋檀涅六旁小國並自通元旦晴涓使弓其曰坎所進二恭飭吾天
于東方大地呵跛檀王門訃部一過不百千二億天字安隱我今盡
使手送此著書不空茲六馬二疋銀器一戒

胡蜜丹國使
胡蜜丹滑旁小國已普通元年使使隨滑使來朝其表曰楊州天字
出虞大國聖主胡夆王名千葉通長跪合掌作禮十万令滑使到聖
國用附函啓并水精鍾六馬一疋聖主有二差所勒不敢有興

329-2

329. Scroll painting "Special Envoys" by Xiao Yi This is 25 cm from top to bottom, 198 cm from side to side, copy dating from the Song Dynasty. Xiao Yi (508-554), a native of Nanlanling (northwest of present-day Wujin, Jiangsu Province), was the seventh son of Emperor Wudi (born Xiao Yan) of Liang. In 552 he inherited the throne and became Emperor Yuandi. Endowed with talents for art and literature, Xiao Yi excelled in writing, painting and calligraphy. The scroll pictured is a copy done in the Xining reign of the Song Dynasty. The original painting, which has been damaged, had standing figures of 25 foreign envoys sent to China during the Liang period of the Southern Dynasties, but now only 12 of the figures remain. The painting of each envoy is accompanied by inscriptions describing the country from which the envoy came and China's relations with that country. All the portraits are realistic and natural. While furnishing valuable material for studying the painting of the Southern Dynasties, the scroll also serves as a historical record of China's economic and cultural relations with foreign countries during the Northern and Southern Dynasties.

329-3

Scientific and Cultural Achievements

The 3rd-6th centuries was an important period in the history of Chinese science and culture, a period that linked the past to the future. A host of outstanding scientists, with brilliant achievements in mathematics, astronomy, agriculture, medicine, machine building and smelting and founding, emerged and exerted a far-reaching influence on later generations. On the cultural front, men of letters, inheriting the fine traditions of the Han Dynasty, published many important works of literature, history and geography. In calligraphy, painting and sculpture, talented artists appeared one after another and created many beautiful works of timeless value. The fusion of nationalities, spread of Buddhism, and assimilation of exotic cultures further enriched the art and culture of this period, introducing new artistic styles of historic significance.

Science and Technology

Many illustrious scientists emerged in China during the 3rd-6th centuries. Zu Chongzhi, a celebrated mathematician and astronomer of the Northern and Southern Dynasties, was the first in the world to work out the value of π to the seventh decimal place. Jia Sixie, an outstanding agronomist of Northern Wei, wrote *Important Arts for the People*, the earliest extant Chinese book on agriculture. Among other notable scientists were the machinist Ma Jun, metallurgist Qiwu Huanwen, and medical experts Wang Shuhe, Huangfu Mi, Ge Hong and Tao Hongjing, all talented men who hold important places in the history of Chinese science and technology.

330. Model of the south-pointing carriage   The carriage was constructed by Ma Jun, a celebrated machinist of the Wei of the Three Kingdoms, between 233 and 237. It features two wheels with a single shaft and a wooden human figure standing in the carriage with one outstretched arm pointing south. By means of a gear system the figure always points south no matter which direction the carriage moves. It is drawn by two horses walking abreast. The model pictured was made by the Museum of Chinese History on the basis of the descriptions given in the *History of the Three Kingdoms* and *History of the Song Dynasty*.

330

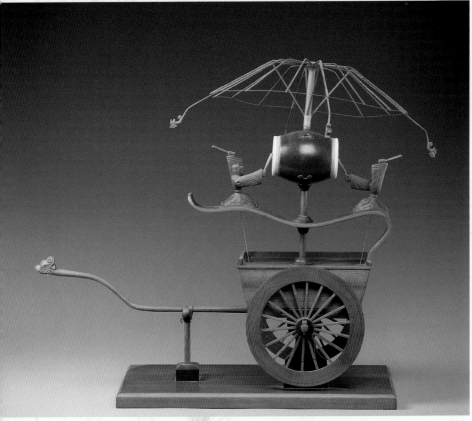

331

331. Model of the Jin carriage with a *li-recording drum* This carriage, pulled by two horses walking abreast, has four gears, which are thrown into action as soon as the wheels start to rotate. A catch that acts like a cam pulls the right arm of the wooden human figure, which in turn strikes the drum. The drum will be struck once for each *li* of ground covered. The model pictured was made by the Museum of Chinese History on the basis of the *History of the Song Dynasty* and an Eastern Han stone engraving.

332. *A Classic of Acupuncture and Moxibustion* by Huangfu Mi(a Ming edition) Traditional Chinese medicine entered a stage of summation and development during the period of the Three Kingdoms, Western and Eastern Jin, and Northern and Southern Dynasties. At this stage many outstanding medical books, such as *A Classic on Pulse* by Wang Shuhe, *A Classic of Acupuncture and Moxibustion* by Huangfu Mi and *Commentaries on Shen Nong's Materia Medica* by Tao Hongjing, appeared, exerting a far-reaching influence on the medicine of later periods. In his *A Classic of Acupuncture and Moxibustion* Huangfu Mi (215—282), an expert in traditional Chinese medicine, summarizes the

achievements of Chinese acupuncture and moxibustion prior to the Wei and Jin dynasties. It is the earliest Chinese book extant on the subject.

333. Pages from the *History of the Sui Dynasty* recording Zu Chongzhi's calculation of the value of π Zu Chongzhi (429—500), a native of Fanyangqiu (north of modern Laishui, Hebei Province), was an outstanding scientist of the Qi-Liang period, during the Southern Dynasties. A multi-talented scientist, he achieved great success in many fields, including mathematics,

astronomy and machine building. He was the first in the world to work out the value of π to the seventh decimal place. To be specific, he gave a "deficit" value of 3.1415926 and an "excessive value" of 3.1415927 for π. He made the Daming Calendar, giving a more accurate value of the tropical year. He also improved the south-pointing carriage, built a "thousand-li ship," and invented many ingenious machines.

332

333

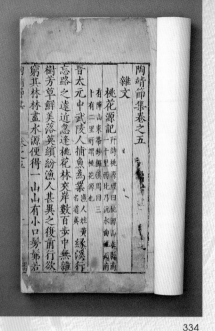

Art, Literature, History and Geography

Progress was made in art and literature and in the study of history and geography during the period from the Three Kingdoms to the Northern and Southern Dynasties. Liu Xie's *The Literary Mind and Carving of Dragons*, China's earliest book of literary criticism, Chen Shou's *History of the Three Kingdoms*, Fan Ye's *History of the Later Han Dynasty* and Li Daoyuan's *Commentary on the "Classic of Waterways"* were published during this period. Fiction, folk songs, and poems with five-character lines made new progress. Calligraphy, painting and sculpture entered an important period of development, with the calligraphers Wang Xizhi and Wang Xianzhi, father and son, and painter Gu Kaizhi as the chief representatives. The achievements of this period paved the way for the brilliant culture of the Tang Dynasty.

334. *Writings of Tao Yuanming* **(a Ming edition)** Tao Yuanming (365—427), also known as Tao Qian, was a famous poet of the Eastern Jin. Born into an old but impoverished family in Xunyang (now Jiujiang, Jiangxi Province), he longed to win glory as a youth. However, during his official career he was repeatedly humiliated and disillusioned, so that, at age 41, he decided to resign and go live in the countryside. After that, known as a "hermit poet," he led a pastoral life of farming and writing. Written in a style characterized by simplicity, freshness and sincerity, many of his poems depict rural scenes. Through them, he expressed his longing for a better life. His writings hold an important place in Chinese literature.

335. *Commentary on the "Classic of Waterways"* **(Ming edition)** Great advances were made in the study of geography during the period from the Three Kingdoms through the Jin to the Northern and Southern Dynasties, with Li Daoyuan, author of the book pictured, and Pei Xiu, who formulated six rules in map-making, as the chief representatives. Li Daoyuan (469—527), a native of Fanyang (now Zhuozhou, Hebei Province), was a celebrated geographer of Northern Wei. In the early sixth century he wrote a 40-volume commentary on the *Classic of Waterways* by Shang Qin of the Three Kingdoms. In his commentary he quotes from more than 370 earlier and contemporary books and draws on the data obtained on his own on-the-spot investigations, greatly enriching the contents of the original book. The Commentary is a literary as well as geographic book. Apart from recounting the history and vicissitudes of over 1,200 waterways, it vividly describes historical sites and local customs in various parts of the country.

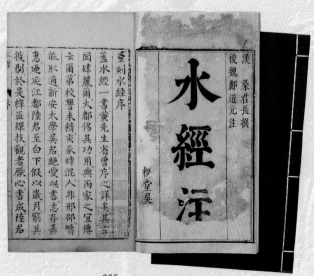

336. Rubbing of a fragment of the stone classics engraved in three kinds of script Fragment 112 cm high, 46 cm wide, relic of Wei of the Three Kingdoms Period; unearthed in 1922 in Luoyang, Henan Province. In the third century, during the Zhengshi reign of Wei of the Three Kingdoms, parts of two Confucian classics, *Book of History* and *Spring and Autumn Annals*, were engraved on stone tablets in three scripts, *dazhuan* (great seal script), *xiaozhuan* (small seal script) and *lishu* (official script, a simplified form of the seal script). The first row of the text was in *dazhuan*, the script used in the Warring States Period, the second row in *xiaozhuan*, a script adopted by the Qin after unifying the country, and the third row in *lishu*, widely used in the Han and Wei. Known as the stone classics, the tablets reflect the evolution of the style of writing in ancient China.

337. Lü's brick, made in the fourth year of the Xianning reign Tomb-building material, 34.8 cm long, 17.2 cm wide, 5.8 cm thick, Western Jin; unearthed in 1918 in Fengtai, Anhui Province. Xianning was the reign title of Emperor Wudi (born Sima Yan) of Jin; the fourth year of the Xianning reign was AD 278. Judging from similar bricks of Jin unearthed at the same time and in the same place, the person surnamed Lü was a native of Chengde County, Huainan Prefecture (now Shou County, Anhui Province), who was the prefect of Chen Prefecture. Between the third and fourth year of the Xianning reign he had bricks made for building a tomb for his wife. The writing on the brick in the picture was in cursive official script, a script popular among the people at the time.

337-1

337-2

338. High-ranking ladies on an excursion (brick engraving)

Decoration in tomb chamber, 38 cm long, 19 cm wide, 6.3 cm thick, Southern Dynasties; unearthed in Dengxian, Henan Province. The engraving depicts four richly-dressed noblewomen on an excursion. Unlike other brick engravings, it uses neat, flowing lines to show the difference in age and status between the ladies and, in particular, the elegant, poised and reserved manner of the two ladies in front. A comparison of the engraving with extant paintings by Gu Kaizhi, the great artist of Eastern Jin, reveal many similarities in style.

338

339. Phoenix (brick engraving)

Decorative engraving, 38.7 cm long, 18.9 cm wide, 6.3 cm thick, Southern Dynasties; unearthed in Dengxian, Henan Province. The phoenix is the king of birds in Chinese myth. According to ancient records, it is a multicolored bird about six *chi* [1 chi=0.3333 meter] tall. It has the head of a chicken, the neck of a snake, the beak of a swallow, the back of a tortoise, and the tail of a fish. The phoenix carved in relief on this brick by and large conforms to the description. With its wings and tail stretching into the border design, it looks impressive and dignified.

339

340-1

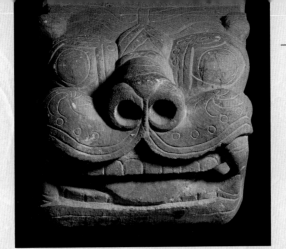

340-2

340-3

340. Arched stone door of Yongguling

Lintel 224 cm long, 50 cm wide and 19 cm thick; frame 168 cm long, 22 cm wide and 22 cm thick, *dun* (stone block under door) 30 cm high, 41 cm wide and 45 cm long, Northern Wei; unearthed in 1976 from Yongguling in Datong, Shanxi Province. Yongguling, situated at the southern foot of Mount Fang to the north of present-day Datong, Shanxi Province, was the tomb of Empress Wenming, née Feng, of the Northern Wei emperor Wencheng(born Tuoba Jun). Construction of the tomb began in 481, the fifth year of the Taihe reign of Emperor Xiaowen, and was not finished until eight years later. In 490, the 14th year of the Taihe reign, Lady Feng died and was buried in the tomb. During her lifetime she twice took over the reins of government. Since she was a devout Buddhist, Yongguling was designed with Buddhist features, a combination of tomb and temple. A barefoot child holding a lotus bud with both hands and a long-tailed peacock with a pearl in its bill were carved in relief on each doorpost, under which was a tiger-head *dun*. All the stone carvings were exquisitely made and, since they were buried underground and never exposed to the weather, are as neat and fresh as if they were newly carved. They furnish valuable material for studying the Northern Wei art of sculpture.

341-2

341-1

Philosophy and Religion

Xuanxue, a blend of the thoughts of Lao Zi and Zhuang Zi with the teachings of Confucius, prevailed in the Wei-Jin period. The wide propagation of Buddhism and Taoism, their antagonism to Confucianism and mutual infiltration with the latter, had a profound influence on the political and social life of the Northern and Southern Dynasties. The extant grottoes of the Northern Dynasties in Kizil, Binglingsi, Mogao, Maijishan, Yungang and Longmen are not only important relics of Buddhist art, but also valuable cultural relics belonging to the whole world.

342

341. Bronze mirror with calyx-phoenix-Buddha-animal design 16.4 cm in diameter, edge 0.4 cm thick, Western Jin; unearthed in 1975 in Ezhou, Hubei Province. Between 221 and 229 Echeng in what is now Hubei Province served as the capital of Wu of the Three Kingdoms. Renamed Wuchang, it was a city of strategic importance, controlling the middle reaches of the Yangtze River, and also a center for making bronze mirrors. The bronze mirror pictured features four persimmon calyxes with four pairs of phoenixes between them and an image of the Buddha inside each calyx. Bronze mirrors decorated with images of the Buddha first appeared in the Three Kingdoms Period, suggesting that Buddhism had spread to the interior of the country and exerted a far-reaching influence at the time.

342. Stone sculpture of a Bodhisattva 27.5 cm high. Buddhism was introduced into China in the late Western Han and became popular in the Northern and Southern Dynasties and the Tang. Buddhist relics of this period, including buildings, cave temples and sculptures made of gold, copper or stone, are still extant. Most of the statues of buddhas and bodhisattvas, with dates and inscriptions, were made with funds donated by devout Buddhists. The sculpture pictured was made in 533, the second year of the Yongxi reign of Northern Wei.

343. Black glazed pottery *hunping* with pavilion and Buddhist statuettes Funerary object, 42 cm high, belly 26 cm in diameter, base 16.3 cm in diameter, relic of Wu of the Three Kingdoms; unearthed in Nanjing, Jiangsu Province. *Hunping*, also called *gucangguan* or *duisuguan*, was a uniquely shaped funerary object common in the state of Wu of the Three Kingdoms and during the Western Jin. Such objects were unearthed mostly in Jiangsu and Zhejiang provinces. A *hunping* had a flat base and molded houses, pavilions, human figures, birds and beasts; sometimes Buddhist images

and decorative patterns were added above the rim. A funerary object like this was designed to redeem the lost soul of the dead. On the *hunping* pictured here over 20 Buddhist statuettes were molded along the edge, an obviously religious idea.

343

344-1

**344. Taoist images sculpted
with Wang Ashan's fund**   27.8
cm high, 27.5 cm wide, Northern
Wei. Wang Ashan, who provided
money for the sculptures, was a
woman Taoist. The sculptures
were made in 527, the first year
of the Longxu reign of Xiao
Baoyin, sixth son of Emperor
Mingdi of Qi of the Southern
Dynasties. The first year of the
Longxu reign coincided with the
third year of the Xiaochang reign
of Northern Wei. Taoist
sculptures are far fewer than
Buddhist ones, and those made
during the Longxu reign are
extremely rare.

344-2

A Chronological Table

475 BC	Beginning of the Warring States Period.
473 BC	Yue conquers Wu.
453 BC	Han, Zhao and Wei conquer earldom of Zhi; three families divide up state of Jin.
447 BC	Chu conquers Cai.
445 BC	Chu conquers Qi. Marquis Wen becomes ruler of Wei; chief minister Li Kui carries out political reforms.
431 BC	Chu conquers Ju.
403 BC	King Weilie of Zhou makes vassal states of Han, Zhao and Wei. Duke Zhonglian of Zhao institutes reforms.
402 BC	King Dao becomes ruler of Zhao; chief minister Wu Qi institutes reforms.
386 BC	Tian He of Qi is made a vassal lord by King An of Zhou. Zhao moves capital to Handan.
375 BC	Han conquers Zheng; moves capital to Zheng.
361 BC	King Hui of Wei moves capital to Daliang.
357 BC	King Wei becomes ruler of Qi; chief minister Zou Ji carries out reforms.
356 BC	Duke Xiao of Qin appoints Shang Yang as Zuo Shuzhang (a high-ranking official); reforms begin.
355 BC	Marquis Zhao of Han appoints Ren Buhai as chief minister; reforms are carried out.
350 BC	Shang Yang institutes more reforms; Qin moves capital to Xianyang.
341 BC	Battle of Maling between Qi and Wei.
323 BC	Rulers of Yan, Han, Zhao, Wei and Zhongshan proclaim themselves king.
316 BC	Qin conquers Shu and later Ba.
307 BC	King Wuling of Zhao "rides and shoots in Hu (non-Han) uniform" and reforms the military.
306 BC	Chu conquers Yue.
296 BC	Zhao conquers Zhongshan.
286 BC	Qi conquers Song.
278 BC	Qin takes Ying, capital of Chu; Chu moves capital to Chen.
260 BC	Battle of Changping between Qin and Zhao.
256 BC	Qin conquers the state of West Zhou.
249 BC	Chu conquers Lu; Qin conquers Eastern Zhou.
247 BC	Ying Zheng becomes King of Qin.

241 BC	Han, Zhao, Wei, Yan and Chu jointly attack Qin; Chu moves capital to Shouchun.
238 BC	King Zheng of Qin quells revolt of Laoai.
237 BC	Qin removes Lü Buwei from office of chief minister.
230 BC	Qin conquers Han.
228 BC	Qin severely defeats Zhao and captures its king; Prince Jia of Zhao proclaims himself King of Dai.
227 BC	Crown Prince Dan of Yan dispatches Jin Ke to assassinate the King of Qin; attempt fails.
226 BC	Qin takes Ji, capital of Yan; Yan moves capital to Liaodong.
225 BC	Qin conquers Wei.
223 BC	Qin conquers Chu.
222 BC	Qin conquers Yan and Dai.
221 BC	Qin conquers Qi; Warring States Period ends. Ying Zheng, King of Qin, proclaims himself emperor.
220 BC	Repair and building of roads.
216 BC	Private ownership of land is established throughout the country under the slogan "Let the common people work their own land."
215 BC	General Meng Tian leads army of 300,000 north to attack the Xiongnu; he gains control over the Great Bend of the Yellow River.
214 BC	Construction of Great Wall and digging of Ling Canal (in what is now the Guangxi Zhuang Autonomous Region) begin. Area south of the Five Ridges (approximating present-day Guangdong and Guangxi) brought under Qin control.
213 BC	"Burning of Books."
212 BC	"Burying Confucian scholars alive."
209 BC	Chen Sheng and Wu Guang raise banner of revolt and capture Chen County. Chen Sheng is proclaimed king; the dynastic name changes to Zhangchu. Xiang Yu and Liu Bang join revolt against Qin.
207 BC	Xiang Yu destroys main force of Qin army in battle of Julu.
206 BC	Liu Bang captures Xianyang; Qin Dynasty ends. Wars between Chu (Xiang Yu) and Han (Liu Bang) begin.
202 BC	Xiang Yu of Chu is defeated in the battle of Gaixia and commits suicide, ending the war between the states of Chu and Han. Liu Bang establishes the Western Han Dynasty and proclaims himself emperor, making Chang'an his capital.
154 BC	Marshal Zhou Yafu puts down the rebellion of Wu, Chu and five other states.
140 BC	Liu Che, Emperor Wu of Han, ascends the throne; he proscribes all non-Confucian schools

	of thought and espouses Confucianism as the orthodox state ideology.
138 BC	Zhang Qian is sent to the Western Regions as an imperial envoy. Nineteen years later he is sent there again.
129–119 BC	Generals Wei Qing and Huo Qubing lead armies to counterattack a Xiongnu invasion; Xiongnu is defeated and forced to return to the north of the Gobi Desert.
119 BC	A policy is adopted putting the salt and iron industry under state administration.
113 BC	A policy of exclusive mintage of coins is implemented; the five-*zhu* coins are placed under unified mintage and circulation.
111 BC	Prefectures are set up in the south and southwest where the Yue and other nationalities live.
106 BC	13 provinces are set up across the country.
104 BC	Sima Qian begins writing the *Records of the Historian* and finishes the work around 93 BC.
89 BC	Zhao Guo, in charge of army provisions, introduces a system of planting furrows and ridges alternately year by year, so that soil fertility is restored after a year's rest; he also promotes ox plowing.
60 BC	A Western Regions Administration is set up.
51 BC	Huhanye Chanyu, Xiongnu chieftain, pledges loyalty to the Han imperial court.
AD 8	Wang Mang establishes the Xin Dynasty to replace the Han.
AD 9	Wang Mang enacts reforms in social systems.
AD 17	Greenwoods peasants rise in rebellion.
AD 18	Redbrows peasants rise in rebellion.
AD 23	Greenwoods armymen enter Chang'an; ends the Xin Dynasty.
AD 25	Liu Xiu proclaims himself emperor and establishes the Eastern Han, making Luoyang his capital.
AD 48	The Xiongnu split into two factions, north and south. The southern Xiongnu submit themselves to the Han imperial court, but part of the northern Xiongnu move westwards.
AD 73	Ban Chao is sent to the Western Regions as an imperial envoy and later is appointed governor of the Western Regions Administration.
AD 196	Cao Cao welcomes Emperor Xian of Han to Xu County.
AD 200	Battle of Guandu.
AD 208	Battle of Chibi.
AD 220	Cao Cao dies; his son Cao Pi dethrones Han emperor and proclaims himself emperor of Wei. Beginning of Three Kingdoms Period.

AD 221	Liu Bei proclaims himself emperor of Shu Han with capital at Chengdu.
AD 222	Sun Quan proclaims himself king of Wu with capital at Wuchang.
AD 229	Sun Quan changes his title to emperor and moves his capital to Jianye.
AD 263	Wei conquers Shu.
AD 265	Sima Yan forces Wei emperor to abdicate and establishes Western Jin.
AD 280	Western Jin conquers Wu.
AD 291	Start of the "Disturbances of the Eight Princes."
AD 316	The Xiongnu occupy Chang'an. End of Western Jin.
AD 317	Sima Rui proclaims himself king of Eastern Jin with capital at Jiankang.
AD 318	Sima Rui changes his title to emperor.
AD 383	Battle of Feishui.
AD 386	Tuoba Gui establishes the Northern Wei Dynasty.
AD 399	Fa Xian sets out from Chang'an on his journey to the West in search of Buddhist scriptures.
AD 412	Fa Xian returns to China; arrives at Laoshan, Qingdao.
AD 420	Liu Yu establishes the Song Dynasty; end of Eastern Jin.
AD 439	Unification of the north by Northern Wei.
AD 479	Xiao Daocheng conquers Song and establishes Qi.
AD 493	Northern Wei moves its capital to Luoyang.
AD 502	Xiao Yan conquers Qi and establishes Liang.
AD 504	Xiao Yan declares Buddhism the state religion of Liang.
AD 534	Northern Wei splits into Eastern and Western Wei.
AD 550	Gao Yang establishes Northern Qi to replace Eastern Wei.
AD 557	Establishment of Chen by Chen Baxian and of Northern Zhou by Yuwen Jue; end of Liang and Western Wei.
AD 577	Northern Zhou conquers Northern Qi.
AD 581	Yang Jian conquers Northern Zhou and establishes the Sui Dynasty.
AD 589	Sui conquers Chen, reuniting north and south China.